Editorial

When Peter Usborne, the children's publisher, died earlier this year his daughter Nicola, who is his successor, said, 'He was always going to be involved until the very end. He was a pretty amazing boss. Of course, his plan was never to die.'

Of course, his plan was never to die. I know people like that.

His publishing business began in the same year as *PN Review* whose editor shares Usborne's plan, even though for at least the last dozen years 'succession planning' has been an agenda item at every Carcanet/*PN Review* board meeting, a nod in the direction of the unpunctual Reaper. The SWOT analysis we produce for the audit foregrounds the general editor as the strength, weakness, opportunity and threat of the operation.

When I discovered, due to a careless leak, that a celebration of the magazine and its editor, in the form of a supplement, was planned for this issue, to be insinuated into it without me knowing, I was alarmed, though also moved in a dozen ways – to gratitude for the initiative of my fellow editors; for the rich content of the supplement, which I saw in proof; and to a sense of puzzlement. Is the fact that someone has stuck in the same job for fifty years a matter of celebration or ought it not rather to be an occasion for pity: how lazy he must be never to have ventured into the wider world, how little imagination he must have to mark the biggest revolutions in his life by an adjustment of the cover design or an alteration in formatting.

Other more self-forgiving thoughts followed: that the magazine has always been (and continues to be) a collaboration between me and named and unnamed co-editors, several of them generous contributors to the supplement in this issue and dear friends old and new. The supplement is full of anecdotes which remind me that few days passed without intellectual engagement and conflict, few without laughter. And it struck me that the 'I' who is writing this editorial note is not the same 'I' who pompously wrote the first, in his best impersonal voice, fifty years ago:

> The need has arisen in the last few years for a magazine that expresses and explores the growing consensus among poets and readers of poetry – a consensus which can be traced in the critical writing of authors as different as John Bayley, Donald Davie, and Terry Eagleton; in the poetries of Charles Tomlinson, Geoffrey Hill, C. H. Sisson, Philip Larkin, and others. There is a renewed popularity and practice of clearly formal writing, a common bridling at vacuous public and private rhetoric, and at the same time a refusal – confronted with the variety and rich potential of new poetic modes – to surrender catholicity and assume the too readily available stance of the embattled poet or critic. The writers who most interest us as editors differ widely in their views of what the ends of poetry should be, but a substantial agreement exists in their view of the means: the necessary intelligence that must be brought to the poetic act (whether of writing or of reading), the shaping of adequate forms, and, equally important, the responsibilities to a vital linguistic and formal heritage, to a living language, to a living community.

That same 'I' was soon to learn that the Republic of Letters (which the title *Poetry Nation* was intended to evoke, rather than a narrowly English focus) included women, and writers from other Englishes and different ethnicities, and wrested into English from other languages (not just the Classics). Some of the jolts that altered the direction of the editorial 'I' may have begun with John Ash, who led to John Ashbery and the wide wake he drew behind him; it included Sujata Bhatt, who opened my ears to other Englishes, and Eavan Boland and her advocacies. And it continued from there. My love for the poets and prose writers I started from editorially remains undiminished, but I now love poets – poetries – they would and could never have done.

The I who writes this editorial is uncomfortable in the company of the ur-I, author of that first one. An old man refuses to revise his youthful work because the young man he was would have hated the old man he has become as much as the old man resents the youth he was. *Resent* is too strong a word. *Comprehends* might be better, because he sees, as the young man could not, all the wrong turnings and wrong decisions taken. But there are also in the rich archive of this magazine an abundance of right directions, many astonishments, discoveries, and, most remarkably, rediscoveries. Readers should never stop looking over their shoulders, or forget that they have two shoulders to look over, even as they proceed gingerly along the road of the present which is scarily deep in things that describe themselves as poems. One might one day get lost in a drift of them.

Letters

Emma Tristram writes: I can't help noticing that in issue 270, Philip Terry quotes Villon's line (in translation) as 'But where are all the snows of yesteryear?'. It took me years to realise that 'Mais ou sont les neiges d'antan' was an iambic tetrameter, with 'nei-ges' as a two-syllable word. Rossetti's version, 'But where are the snows of yesteryear' is almost one too, as it has one extra syllable. By adding 'all' to that, Terry has changed it into an iambic pentameter. It has become rather ponderous and too regular, losing the lightness of melting snow. Is this an example of the tendency of iambic tetrameters to change into iambic pentameters when put into English?

Perhaps this was just a mistake. But then I saw 'Ita missa', as a sentence on its own, in Colm Tóibín's poem 'A United Ireland'. The usual phrase is 'Ite missa est', once the last phrase of the Latin mass, usually translated as 'Go, the Mass is ended'. (Wikipedia suggests the phrase, whatever it means, dates back to the third century and may be the origin of the word 'missa' to describe the Mass.) Is 'ita' a mistake, or a play on words, 'Thus, the

Mass'? Or is he quoting a misquotation (apparently there is a song by The Power called 'Ita Missa Est')? Having logged the Villon as a mistake, I tend to see 'Ita missa' as one too and so may be missing something.

A convent education made me stumble over this phrase. But I am finding a use for Latin. I know the words of the ordinary mass, and their meaning, by heart, since I have sung them as part of a church choir most Sundays for decades. I have recently put in the 'underlay', i.e. fitting the words to the music, in a mass setting by Josquin des Prez as part of the making of an edition to be played on viols. The sources are not very explicit about how the words should fit. There may be fewer and fewer people who understand those words, and can therefore love the music for the way it sets them. But being played on viols, with the words appearing in the score below the notes, with a translation, gives the music a new life (I hope).

The mass will appear under the imprint 'Particular Music' which has many editions of sixteenth-century vocal music for playing on viols or other instruments.

News & Notes

Among avocado blossoms • *John Robert Lee writes*: My friend Alwin Bully, who has died aged seventy-four in his home island of Dominica, after battling Parkinson's for many years, was a 'renaissance' figure of the Caribbean. He came of age in the dynamic 1970s when so much was happening in the region – in the arts and culture, popular music, politics, literature, ideas. He was the leader among us, excelling as an actor, dancer, playwright, director, painter, sculptor, carnival designer, film actor and director – and designer of Dominica's flag.

We first met in 1969 when, as a student, his University of the West Indies (UWI) theatre group came to St Lucia from Barbados: directing and playing the lead role, he was brilliant, and I was captivated by his huge youthful talent. When I arrived at the same university I joined the drama group that Alwin led. Thus began our friendship. We shared the dreams of mentors including Derek Wal-

cott and Kamau Brathwaite for the growth of Caribbean arts, literature and theatre.

Alwin was born in the centre of Roseau, the capital of Dominica (home of Jean Rhys). His family and especially his cousin Mabel Cissie Caudeiron, who is credited with inspiring a roots revival in Dominican music and culture, were early influences.

He was educated at the Dominica Grammar School (where, later, he became acting principal) and St Mary's Academy before leaving for university in Barbados and graduating in 1972. (In 2011, UWI awarded him an Honorary Doctorate of Letters.)

Returning home in 1972, Alwin founded the People's Action Theatre and was its artistic director until 1987. The group's work marked some of the most productive years in Dominican theatre.

When Dominica became independent in 1978, he

became the first director of the new Department of Culture. In 1987, he moved to Jamaica, to work at UNESCO as Senior Programme Specialist and later as its Caribbean Culture Advisor. Back home in 2008, he became advisor to the Minister of Culture.

He wrote and directed films, including his last production, *Oseyi and the Masqueraders* (2017) – a story after his own heart about a boy's relationship with his village's carnival rituals. By then he was already ill, but he was still working two years ago, dictating a final short story to his wife Anita for his collection *The Cocoa Dancer and Other Stories*.

Alwin Bully was kind and generous, with an unflappable personality, ready smile and easy laughter. He remains a seminal influence in my life. Now, I write in an elegy for him, 'I must catch the ferry to his island, I must wear my shades for the glare off heaving waters of the channel'.

Anita, whom he married in 1977, survives him, along with his daughter Sade and son Brent. Another son, Peron, predeceased him. His sister Barbara Bully-Thomas and brother Colin live in Dominica.

Masquerader fallen
(for A.B. 1948–2023)

Among avocado blossoms, gospelling yellow-breasts –

he died, companion of my youth,
star of stages, late-night laughter,

irrepressible visions – around golden-brown mango blossoms
white butterflies sign algorithms of infinity – under red lilies,
their erect stamens, fallen masqueraders

of banana trees, *pay banan, sensay* – his eyes closed.
his heart stopped. he is over.
the rose of sharon near my stairs has bled bright pink

under an overcast sky, chilling air,
a dog howling, howling at something –

I must catch the ferry to his island, I must wear my shades for the glare
off heaving waters of the channel –

All his women friends and mistresses • *Nicolas Tredell writes*: The novelist, essayist and editor Philippe Sollers died in Paris on 5 May 2023 aged eighty-six. Sollers (originally Joyaux) was born on 28 November 1936 into a well-off family in the city of Talence, near Bordeaux. Destined to run his father's factory, he studied economics at first, but then embarked on a literary career under the aegis of the poet Francis Ponge. In 1957, his short story 'Le Défi' appeared in the journal *Écrire* under his adopted surname 'Sollers' (Latin for 'clever, skilful') and won the Prix Fénéon. Both François Mauriac and Louis Aragon praised his first novel, *Une curieuse solitude* (1958), and three innovative fictions followed: *Le parc* (1961), *Drame* (1965) and *Nombres* (1968). His greatest impact, however, came through the magazine *Tel Quel* [*As Is*] that he co-founded in 1960. Stephen Heath, now Professor of French and English Literature and Culture at Cambridge University, knew Sollers well and, interviewed in *PNR* 83, judged *Tel Quel* 'one of the great avant-garde literary reviews of the twentieth century in its influence and the quality of its writing'. But the original *Tel Quel* project of fusing literary and political revolution broke down, in Heath's view, because of the 'romantic Maoism to which [it] became attached, the whole self-confirming investment in China and the cultural revolution'. This investment collapsed after *Tel Quel*'s 1974 visit to China.

The novelist Christine Brooke-Rose, resident in Paris in the 1960s, was more sceptical about the magazine when interviewed in *PNR* 75: 'I don't think we should take that *Tel Quel* phase too seriously'. She pointed out that by the 1980s, Sollers had 'gone back to writing completely mimetic novels', as exemplified by the bestselling *Femmes* (1983), which is about 'all his women friends and mistresses' (Sollers had married the feminist theorist Julia Kristeva in 1967 and they had one son, David Joyaux). In 1983, after *Tel Quel* had closed, Sollers founded the journal *L'Infini*, which, as its title suggests, took an interest in religion and mysticism that he would pursue throughout his life and which emerges in later novels such as *Une vie divine* (2006), which pitches Nietzsche against Schopenhauer, Yea-Saying against Nay-Saying, and inclines towards the former. In later life, Sollers kept a lower public profile and would never regain the heights of *Tel Quel*, but his considerable *oeuvre* shows, throughout its ideological variations, a constant interest in language in relation to philosophy and ethics.

A very long poem • It is sometimes forgotten that the celebrated novelist D.M. Thomas, author of *The White Hotel* (1982), who has died at the age of eighty-eight, was a poet. 'I've decided I'm a poet who sometimes writes novels,' he affirmed, 'rather than a novelist who used to write poetry.' The fiction is better remembered than the poems. American readers and critics took up *The White Hotel* after its modest English success, and it sold over a million in paperback and 100,000 hardbacks. This success was beamed back to the UK where it was shortlisted for the Booker but pipped at the post by *Midnight's Children*.

During National Service, Thomas studied Russian to become an interrogator and fell in love with Russian literature, translating Pushkin, Akhmatova and others and writing a biography, *Alexander Solzhenitsyn: A Century in His Life* (1998), as well as his five Russian novels. He also published several books of poems. His main legacy (beyond his fiction) may prove to be his translations of Russian poetry. Much of his best fiction draws on the lives and deaths of poets: 'my novels follow the creative laws of poetry, based very largely on symbol and image. If I'd have lived two hundred years ago, I'd have written a very long poem instead.' It's as well he didn't.

An Israeli modernist • The Israeli poet Meir Wieseltier has died at the age of eighty-two. He had received many of the big cultural awards of Israel, most notably the Israel Prize for Literature (2000). He went to Israel from Moscow, where he was born, soon after the state was established, eventually making his home in Tel Aviv. Over time, he published more than twenty books of poetry and translations into Hebrew from Russian, English (including Shakespeare) and French. He was a teacher, magazine editor and poet. One award citation characterised 'his outspoken, mixed poetry, which combines political and social rhetoric with existentialist dimensions', and noted his 'modernist' impact on Israeli poetry.

A remarkable acquisition • The Harry Ransom Center at the University of Texas has acquired James Fenton's archive, a remarkable acquisition. When the Elgin Marbles are returned to Greece, perhaps the Fenton papers will be repatriated to – for example – Oxford. 'Fenton's body of work traces the political upheavals of our time, including the regime of Ayatollah Ruhollah Khomeini, the suppression of political protest in China's Tiananmen Square, and Northern Ireland's fratricidal bloodletting.' Even as an undergraduate Fenton was politically alert as a poet and critic. He was also close to some of the most interesting writers of his generation, with whom he conducted correspondences. The Director of the Harry Ransom Center declared, 'In his poems, James Fenton bears witness to the collective traumas of the twentieth century, and for generations to come his poems will be read and reread for the way they transform that experience into art.'

The spirit of Menard • HetMoet Publishing and Menard Press merge, a happy afterlife for a brilliant, eccentric imprint. Menard's founder *Anthony Rudolf writes*: In recent years Menard Press, founded in 1969, has been dormant, although not completely defunct. Running a small press has no longer been a priority for me. I am eighty and hope to spend my remaining years completing books of my own, revising French and Russian translations, collecting my best essays, and working on a few poems. Small presses have a natural life span. Menard was vanishing into the sunset, without fanfare or regret. Then something unexpected occurred: Elte Rauch of HetMoet Publishing in Amsterdam and I had a lot in common. I have to make a big effort to keep up with her: she is a force of nature, and of culture, too: poet, novelist, translator, song-writer, editor, go-between extraordinaire, publisher and, unlike me, possessing a business head.

Half my age, she has plans to publish many titles in the coming years. While available to give advice, I don't want to be consulted about the choice of titles. But, given that we have similar literary tastes and ethical concerns, I know and rejoice that the spirit of Menard will live on. Thus the merger felt right for the best reasons.

This surprising development gives me pleasure. End of story, as Louis Armstrong says in *High Society*. No, beginning of story, as he also says: the story of HetMoet-Menard Press.

Elte Rauch adds: Anthony Rudolf has been a friend and inspiration for many years. Through our connection and conversations I soon became aware of his Menard Press, its literary and ethical narrative as well as its history and legacy. For me to take on Menard Press and integrate it as a sister branch of my Amsterdam-based indie press HetMoet Publishing seemed a natural development of both our personal and professional kinship.

It is not a burden. A true passion rarely is. I am committed to engaging in modernisation and publishing new authors and translations, while keeping Menard's spirit alive and honoured. 'The end is where we start from' (T.S. Eliot).

Words that bring us together • Mererid Hopwood has been awarded the Hay Festival Medal for Poetry 2023. She is the distinguished Professor of Welsh and Celtic Studies at Aberystwyth University. The other laureates this year are author, illustrator and screenwriter Alice Oseman (Medal for Fiction), Ukraine's rock star poet Serhiy Zhadan (Medal for Songwriting) and prize-winning novelist Salman Rushdie (Medal for Prose).

'In accepting this Medal,' Professor Hopwood said, 'looking back there are many whom I would like to thank for their support from the early days. These include friends at Ysgol Farddol Caerfyrddin for the learning, the Talwrn community for the listening, the students for their enthusiasm and Peter Florence and the Hay Festival for the encouragement. Looking forward, I would like to express the hope that all of us who love literature will continue to search for the words that bring us together in peace rather than drive us apart in war.' Professor Hopwood has, in the words of the Festival announcement, 'spent her career weaving connections between language, literature, education and the arts. She joined Aberystwyth University as Professor of Welsh and Celtic Studies in January 2021, and is secretary of Academi Heddwch. For her poetry, she has won the National Eisteddfod of Wales' Chair, Tir na n'Og prize, Crown and Prose Medal and Welsh Book of the Year prize. She is a regular contributor to the Hay Festival, and has taken part in literature festivals in Europe, Asia and South America.' Hopwood is a worthy and richly Welsh recipient. Among earlier recipients, since the award was established in 2012, *PN Review* readers will remember Gillian Clarke (2016), the Austrian poet Evelyn Schlag (2018) and, last year, Robert Minhinnick.

Touch and Mourning

5: Trespasses

ANTHONY (VAHNI) CAPILDEO

Stevie Smith's recording of 'Not Waving but Drowning' punches holes into the sea. In her voicing, the dead man whose 'moaning' pervades the poem speaks the line 'Oh, no no no, it was too cold always' on a rising crescendo that would be at home on the heath in *King Lear*. Poor bare forked animal with the divine right to howl. Less moaning than warning: the environment that cannot be survived is the cold and heartless crowd who speak about him without him. His own 'moaning', an off-rhyme with 'drowning', is all the mourning the dead man will know. The wave-and-sink look of the lineation of the second stanza (second of three) enacts the social isolation that surrounds, perhaps led to, his loss.

> Poor chap, he always loved larking
> And now he's dead
> It must have been too cold for him his heart gave way,
> They said.

The first line is eight syllables long; the second only half that length. The third line is twelve syllables long, taking us 'far out' indeed into the blank of the page. Before Stevie Smith lets the fourth line drop, she pauses, much more than you might expect; much more than at other commas or line breaks. She delivers 'They said' with unashamed judgment, in a sharp tone like her delivery of the word 'dead' in line one of the poem.

Tonally, Smith's performance sets up a vibration that pings back to the beginning, whereby the *saying* that ends the second stanza cuts like the *death* at the very start of the first. Pauses and intensities convey – not exactly consequence, not exactly culpability – but the space through which the lost one's voice has to rise to be heard, which would be an impossible space without the poem and its art of language. You would imagine that a nameless body claimed by the sea, even a hauntingly re-voiced one, remains out of reach; but no. Whether it was a typewriter key driven into paper, or a pen nib, or pencil point, the technology of Stevie Smith's time was tactile. It is through that touch, from mind to hand to what we can read now, that we can become the too-late mourners of the man who stands in for all the overwhelmed and unknown.

The dead pass beyond. The dead one may be likened to a horseman among those on foot, in Margaret Alexiou's study of modern Greek lament. The French words *trépas*, *trépasser* resemble the English word, 'trespass'. Both mean passing beyond something; the tres- or tré- comes from Latin, *trans*. In English, we trespass on property, generally committing a civil offence, sometimes following an ancient right of way, or common sense on Jah's fruitful earth. In French, we die. Yet *trépas*, for me, continues to evoke images of journeying into that country whence no traveller returns. Plurilingualism – living with or between

languages – leads, as ever, to plurilocalism, layering place on place. This generates an associative poetics, no less emotional than etymological, no less imaginary than mapped. *Trépasser*. Going over the edge of this world. Memory sounds Tennyson's 'Crossing the Bar' – and sees faraway sunset and evening star over some familiar horizon. Memory sounds William Cowper's 'The Castaway', like Virginia Woolf's Mr Ramsay intoning mournfully: 'We perish'd, each alone' – but sees and hears no man; re-imagining, instead, the profound silence that attends Woolf's image of the dying Katherine Mansfield putting on a white wreath and leaving the company of her friends; the silence of conversations never to be.

Is death, then, a way of becoming untouchable? Untouchability: a queen of tennis (for example) might be 'untouchable', in the sense of unsurpassed, peerless. Death as leading to perfection? The murderer and rapist's statue tailored in stone or metal, to dominate our lesser, softer comings and goings. The suffocatingly golden eulogy for a fellow sinner. Untouchability: there is also that other sense, of taboo, ritual (religious or class) 'impurity', sometimes leading to quite modern exclusion and murder. Those who have been deemed too far out to go jogging safely in the North American suburbs, or to drink from the upper-caste well in India. My orthodox Hindu family, when my father died, observed the custom of the house being treated as unclean. People visited, especially for the evening readings from sacred texts. However, they did not eat the food of the 'dead house' ('dead' here meaning 'the dead person's house' as well as 'the house touched by death'). Like a cemetery, we were temporarily unclean. Special ceremonial foods, like black sesame balls, were prepared in the house, exclusively for use in ongoing rites, or for the immediate family; sometimes, for the ancestral dead. I cannot offer you food to eat, when one of mine has tasted death.

I hope that readers and critics will become aware of the traces of cultural reference that inevitably make their way into poems in global Englishes. I still have not drawn on such details enough in my work. Nor can I be sure that Katherine Mansfield's visionary wreath – bride of death – was not white jasmine, flower of the ascetic and destroyer god Shiva; perhaps it was, if her contemporaries Leonard Woolf could novelize Sri Lanka, and T.S. Eliot make his wasteland thunder in Sanskrit. Shiva is also the god of ecstatic orgasm. His phallus, or *lingam*, is considered to manifest throughout the earth, for example in stone formations carved over lengthy time by water dripping in caves, or in purposely carved marble, installed in shrines beneath vessels dripping milky liquid onto the holy masculine. The French phrase 'little death', *petite mort*, has become an overly worn English poeticism. It cannot refer only to the shudder and rigours of dying; it must also refer to the annihilation of self, passing through the senses beyond the senses. In other words: death as passing (through touch) beyond touch. We are back at the untouchable, the unreachable.

You cannot 'kill' the other – sever a relationship, sending the other spinning into the realm of total-feeling untouchability, past intimacy denied, conversations-never-to-be – if you are friends, not lovers. When Robert Browning's Eurydice, in a twist on the original myth, begs Orpheus to look at her – even though they are hurrying out of the underworld, and Orpheus looking at her would break the condition set on her freedom and send her away forever among the shades – she treats looking and touching as one. She desires a moment of beholding her lover and being beheld by him.

But give them me, the mouth, the eyes, the brow!
Let them once more absorb me! One look now
Will lap me round for ever, not to pass
Out of its light, though darkness lie beyond:

Hold me but safe again within the bond
Of one immortal look! All woe that was,
Forgotten, and all terror that may be,
Defied, no past is mine, no future: look at me!

I wonder if this might be because – having experienced death by snakebite, crossed the River Styx, and dwelt among the dead – Eurydice would no longer have an equal relationship with Orpheus, if they re-emerged into the light together, with him as her rescuer, but also with him – unlike her – as someone personally ignorant of death. Perhaps she feared a life in which she would age quickly into becoming just his friend, by virtue of being the too-knowledgeable one, contained and framed as the recovered one; not someone of plural life, fluent in the realms of both Zeus and Hades, but the poet's wife, the one about whom he had everything to say. Yet friendship might have been enough to moor Stevie Smith's 'poor chap' to life.

Reports

The World Sounds

CHRISTIAN WIMAN

This may be my favourite poem. In all of poetry, I mean. On some days, of crepuscular mood and need.

At night, by the fire,
The colors of the bushes
And of the fallen leaves,
Repeating themselves,
Turned in the room,
Like the leaves themselves
Turning in the wind.
Yes: but the color of the heavy hemlocks
Came striding.
And I remembered the cry of the peacocks.

The colors of their tails
Were like the leaves themselves
Turning in the wind,
In the twilight wind.
They swept over the room,
Just as they flew from the boughs of the hemlocks
Down to the ground.
I heard them cry – the peacocks.
Was it a cry against the twilight
Or against the leaves themselves
Turning in the wind,
Turning as the flames
Turned in the fire,
Turning as the tails of the peacocks
Turned in the loud fire,

Loud as the hemlocks
Full of the cry of the peacocks?
Or was it a cry against the hemlocks?

Out of the window,
I saw how the planets gathered
Like the leaves themselves
Turning in the wind.
I saw how the night came,
Came striding like the color of the heavy hemlocks
I felt afraid.
And I remembered the cry of the peacocks.
(Wallace Stevens, 'Domination of Black')

I don't know what the poem means, except that it means more than I know. It teaches me nothing, unless the surge of spiritual alertness it sends through my nerves counts as an increment of knowledge.

Spiritual? What other word should one use for a poem about death that makes one feel so alive?

Death? Is that what the poem is about then? In one sense, obviously: the hemlocks, the fear that starts at home (one man's death) but by the end has become cosmic (the death of all human endeavour, I think, the Great No that nibbles at consciousness, that *is*, in some way, consciousness). It means everything, of course, that for the fallen leaves (elegiacally lovely, one assumes), and the crackling fire, and even the dramatic slashes of the peacock tails, there is that *domination of black*.

Or it means almost everything. Music is moral, says Settembrini in *The Magic Mountain*, insofar as it has the power to be both stimulant and narcotic, to wake one up to life and to put one to sleep. 'Domination of Black' seems to me as close as poetry can come to pure music and still be poetry – or at least the sort of poetry that I enjoy, I should say, for there are certainly other poems, including some by Stevens, that more completely slip free from the gravity of actual denotation. Such escape is not possible here, because this poem is conscious. It wakes one up. Thus, moral.

But Settembrini's dichotomy, like all dichotomies, is reductive. The poem both lulls and prods, wakes and sedates. It has the force of a spell or charm.

Wakes one up to what? 'The danger', writes Simone Weil, 'is not lest the soul should doubt whether there is any bread but lest, by a lie, it should persuade itself that it is not hungry.' Poetry attests to this abiding hunger, even when, perhaps especially when, the poet has lost all sense of the source and does nothing but cry out. 'At a time like the present', Weil continues, 'incredulity may be equivalent to the dark night of Saint John of the Cross if the unbeliever loves God, if he is like the child who does not know whether there is bread anywhere, but who cries out because he is hungry.'

Or, in another key: 'Unreal things have a reality of their own, in poetry as elsewhere' (Stevens).

*

Unreal. A slippery word. It can mean false, used to dismiss a movie with plot holes or a sentimental novel. On the other hand, it can mean truer than we knew was possible: *unreal*, the tourist says staring down into the Grand Canyon. In the first instance, we are frustrated and balked. An experience has been denied us, even as it has reminded us that we have had such experiences in the past. In the second, we are seized and enlarged. We are also – insofar as any experience of awe comes with a charge to act upon it, and insofar as an increased capacity for contemplation constitutes action – called.

But Stevens is using the word in a third sense, which in a way fuses the first two. He is referring to the forms that the imagination both perceives and creates. (Any work of true imagination, I would argue, always fuses those two actions.) There is inevitably an element of falseness to these forms, a factitiousness, as Plato suggested. And there is, though not inevitably, a sharp eruption of truth (or, if that word makes you nervous, a sense of enlarged or clarified or salvaged reality), as any experience of genuine art reveals.

Unreal things have a reality of their own. They will exert their force upon you whether or not you recognize them, but only by recognizing them can they become part of the reality that we usually refer to when we say that word. You have to assent to the invisible if you are ever to see it.

Seeing the Invisible is in fact the title of a monograph by the French philosopher Michel Henry on the work of Wassily Kandinsky. Henry believed that abstract art in general, and Kandinsky's work in particular, was not simply a development in the history of art but the formal fruition of the hunger to truly see – and thereby to truly *be* – that has animated every work ever made. Artists were never in pursuit of the physical world per se. They were in pursuit of the force that compelled them to pursue. 'Life', Henry calls it. It's as good a word as any.

Art, if one really reflects on it and makes an exception of the Greeks, has only rarely been concerned with external reality. The world becomes the aim of an activity that ceases to be creative and lapses into representation and imitation only after its initial theme and true interest has been lost. The initial theme of art and its true interest is life. At its outset, all art is sacred, and its sole concern is the supernatural. This means that it is concerned with life – not with the visible but the invisible. Why is life sacred? Because we experience it within ourselves as something we have neither posited nor willed, as something that passes through us without ourselves as its cause – we can only be and do anything whatsoever because we are carried by it. This passivity of life to itself is our pathetic subjectivity – this is the invisible, abstract content of eternal art and painting.

According to Nina Kandinsky, her husband would create special colours for some paintings, colours that had never before existed, which he would then throw away once the painting was completed so that the colour could never be replicated. He didn't do this to create something original *to him*. He did it to honour, to participate in, the eternally dynamic nature of reality. 'The world sounds', Kandinsky wrote. 'It is a cosmos of spiritually affective beings. Thus, dead matter is living spirit.' The most obvious way of reading this thought is that matter is pregnant with spirit. Reality is always in excess of perception, and any work (or life) that does not acknowledge this excess (and this splendid ignorance) is not only missing much of reality, but is itself *unreal* in the worst sense. But there's another implication, which is not necessarily incompatible with this. Kandinsky's image could suggest a sort of claustrophobic finitude: instead of spirit animating and brimming from matter, what if, sometimes, it is trapped within it? Many writers have written about the liberating experience of great art, but what if we are not the only ones being freed? 'The feeling remains', wrote Teresa of Avila, 'that God is on the journey too.'

'Graves, No Cars' – On the roadside, Niue, November 2022

GREGORY O'BRIEN

The dead man disembarks the Air New Zealand flight about the same time as the rest of us, and a good quarter hour before the suitcases follow him across the tarmac. His coffin – first item to leave the hold – is propelled, respectfully, by numerous hands around the side of the terminal and into the shade, bypassing the immigration booths. As this unfolds, the airport's resident roosters and chickens, oblivious to it all, continue their military-style manoeuvres out on the expanse of white coral concrete which is the runway. With only one scheduled weekly flight in and out, there are but two or three hours each week when the tarmac doesn't entirely belong to the poultry and other bird-life.

Today's coffin contains the body of an esteemed member of the Auckland-based Niuean population. (With only 1,500 Niueans now living on the equatorial island, some 95 percent of Niueans live in New Zealand – a three-and-a-half-hour flight south.) The deceased has been accompanied on the flight home by a sizable band of mourners, most of them wearing purple T-shirts bearing his name, 'Papa ...', and his dates of birth and death. Some garments bear his photo-portrait, and prayers in English or Niuean. Alongside the island's modest tourist trade, the northward migration of the dead – usually, as in this case, with entourage – must account for a significant proportion of the island's arrivals by air in any given year.

The graves of Niue are distributed in well-groomed clusters along the verge of the ring-road which encircles the island and is integral to the day-to-day functioning of this, the world's least populous nation. My geographer friend, Robin Kearns, considers the disposition of graves a kind of mapping: an overlay of the afterlife onto the present-day life of the place. A palimpsest. It might even amount to a ghost story if his notion of geography could stretch that far.

The island is awash not only with funerary monuments but with dogs, many of which pass the long, hot days laid out on the grassy strip between graveyard and roadside, their noses warming on the highway which is made of the same iridescent coral as the runway. In one settlement, over a number of days, we are struck by the loyalty of one dog, which is always in attendance at the roofed-over grave of its master. (The tomb is positioned, as is the protocol here, directly in front of the house in which the deceased used to live.)

Our poet/painter friend John Puhiatau Pule moved back to his ancestral land in the village of Liku – where he was born in 1962 – seven years ago. He has six, maybe seven family-members buried between his house and the road or within a minute's walk along the Liku-Hakupu road. Older burial sites on the island rarely have headstones or any form of overt marking. John recently uncovered the site of another family grave after an elderly aunt offered the necessary coordinates. Taking a machete to a clump of all-enveloping vegetation not far from his house, John soon found the tell-tale, albeit scattered, mound of rocks.

An island offers anyone who ventures there a heightened sense of both life and death. That was something I learnt a decade ago, when I spent a few days on New Zealand's northernmost outpost, Raoul Island. Niue is similarly confronting. An island is a lesson. On an earlier visit here – to the 'The Rock of the Pacific', as Niue is often called – I was struck by how closely the island resembled Thomas More's *Utopia* – particularly as it appeared in an engraving by Ambrosius Holbein (reproduced on the cover of the Oxford University Press paperback edition). Instead of a ring-road, however, More's utopian location had a waterway which surged between intricate, well-governed townships, all of which featured prominent church buildings. All very like Niue.

'Like a well-functioning machine or clock in the careful calibration of its parts', I noted in my journal from that trip, 'More's utopian island also bears, in Holbein's rendering, an uncanny resemblance to a human brain or head. So, too, Niue.' Beyond both the island's dogs and its graves, there is an upwelling sense that The Rock has its own percolating intelligence, alongside a paradoxical character and a certain pedagogical inclination.

Lessons of the Alofi – Alofi Highway

Lesson of the overladen coconut palm
Lesson of the westward-tracking frigate bird
Lesson of the unsuspecting roadside dog, nose
   warming on the white coral asphalt
Lesson of the rain wherever it falls
Lesson of the shipping container stacked with
   bottles of wine, all of them spoiled after two days
   left out on Sir Robert's Wharf in sweltering sun
Lesson of Cyclone Heta and the migration of houses
Lesson of the coconut crab crossing the coast road,
   slowly, distractedly
Lesson of the night voices emanating from the
   unpeopled rooms of a house recently built on
   unsanctioned land – a house in which no one will
   ever sleep
Lesson of the slack-tuned guitar, all seventeen frets
   of it, six compliant strings and a jumble of chords
Lesson of learning to read the expression on the face
   of the coconut
Lesson of the car left six months unattended at the
   jungle's edge, now completely dismantled by
   vegetation
Lesson of the headscarf of the deserted wife and the
   island's long tradition of beautiful hats and great
   loss

The ring road is often described as a necklace along

which the villages are strung. It holds the island together, linking its communities, yet also allowing them some breathing room. While the road ducks in and out of the world of the living, it never loses sight of, or touch with, the sentinel dead who rest beneath their road-facing markers. Most of these gravestones are constructed using a concrete compound made of ground-up coral – like both road and runway in this regard. The fading whiteness of the coral is refreshed frequently with lashings of white housepaint which give the memorials an insistent, directional road-signage quality.

'Graves, No Cars' announces a well-weathered sandwich board at one end of Alofi. Travelling from the other direction, it reads: 'No Cars, Graves'. Not only are there actual gravestones adjacent to this impromptu/permanent piece of signage but there are, in all probability, human remains beneath it as well, John tells us. Hence its precise placement, mid-lawn. Another lesson of the island: the earth beneath your feet is ancestrally laden and requires an appropriate respect. *Media vita in morte sumus,* as the Massbook in the Catholic church at Makefu, if consulted, might add.

Alongside the funereal contingent on the Air New Zealand flight, there are nineteen young female and a solitary male veterinarians, all of them volunteers, tasked with sorting out the island's 'dog problem'. (This is the first such programme since the Covid pandemic shut the island down in early 2020.) Their twelve-day mission, they tell us brightly, is to desex as good a proportion of the canine population as they can manage. A handwritten sign outside the clinic speaks plainly enough: 'Working Together. We Desex Them You Register Your Dogs.'

Each morning, the young women venture off into the villages, picking up the road- and grave-side canines and taking them back to a disused primary school classroom which has become a temporary dog-operating-theatre. The self-titled 'Rock Vets' and their endeavours struck me at first as the most unpromising and unlikely subject for a poem – but you never can be sure.

Dog Day, Alofi

An interruption to the village music,
the slow, humid doggedness of the day:

a flurry of veterinarians, fresh from the plane and
morning run-around. Plucked

from white coral roadside, the island's quota of
up-ended canines, tail-high in their impromptu
    clinic,

in recovery now, asleep in cages stacked
six by five – like days of a dog-calendar –

the name of their village, handwritten, taped to the
    forehead
of each. Short-lived tranquillity of the post-operative
    pack.

Late afternoon, the length of the reverberating
    ring-road,
the settlements resume their dog-barking,
    car-chasing ways.

The dead do not travel anywhere fast. Neither do the living – they go quietly, slowly about their island lives. A Pacific frigate bird – the Niuean national bird – flickers across the sky directly above the schoolroom where the dogs are slowly finding their way back to consciousness... The fecund, tropical atmosphere envelops all of it.

In contrast to the well-mown rectangles of lawn surrounding the graves, the tropical forest is tumultuous and anarchic. We marvel at how a late-model car left parked on the edge of the bush can, within a few months, be busted open and taken apart by a considerable number of plant-species, working as a team. A great many uninhabited dwellings around the island have been similarly reclaimed by bush, by trees growing up through the floorboards, filling the rooms then nonchalantly lifting off the roofs.

The bush. The road. The graves. The dogs. The dead car. And then there is the rain, bucketing down, but seldom staying for long. The rain – the daily downpour – is probably the island's brashest theatrical production. It renders the entire place sodden and glistening, its inhabitants alternatively bedraggled and euphoric. And then, as if on cue, the sun reappears and within ten minutes there is no trace of it ever having rained.

The fecundity of the tropical island, with its tempests, hurricanes and flash-floods, also presents as a kind of delirium or intoxication. Maybe the reason we go to remote islands is for an inversion – or is it more of an amplification – of the actual, the accustomed? An island is a place where nature can be deafeningly loud and humanity uncharacteristically quiet. And where the living inhabitants are vastly outnumbered not only by dogs and chickens but by the memorialised dead. Even the rain on the island of Niue feels different – falling on and through everything, and becoming itself a part of everything. You can see the long lines of rain approaching from across the horizon and closing in on the island. Lines of rain – sentences, paragraphs, chapters, entire books. Lists of names, inventories, chronologies and genealogies dangling from the greyness above. A gathering together and then a great letting go. Everything drawn up into the monsoon sky, then returned almost at once to its place of origin.

Downpour, Namukulu

A rare bird, funeral procession, the rain
  worn as headdress. The rain my second body.
Rain my cousin, my niece
rain that admires its reflection in a pond
rain that is a satellite of itself
a language I struggle to speak.

Rain tattooed on arms and shoulders
the cut of its cloth, fall of its jacket
    a week of Sundays. The upstanding rain
on the upside-down furniture of Vaiolama.

Rain in memory, in servitude, in loss and gain.
The rain a machete hacking its way through a forest
rain that enters through eyes, nostrils, ears and
    mouth
    rain that never leaves.

Rain on the tomb of the fourteen Niuean infantry-
    men
    lost in World War One
rain I wrap around me like a towel. A language
  I have trouble remembering. Rain falling upon
Bob Marley and the Wailers
                    playing from a boombox in a
    derelict house.
Lengthy dictation of rain on an iron rooftop
    the sea-slug admiring, but hardly interested.

The rain an upended tray. Rain on the coral runway
    on Flight 957 bound for Auckland. Rain that will
    give
    the coconut crab no rest, on the road to Avatele
rain on the baubles and trappings of empire
    rain I wrap around me like a shroud

rain on the street lamps of Namukulu
    if only there were streets, lamps –
rain on the hillside of Namukulu
    if only you were with me in Namukulu.

Thanks to Robin Kearns and the School of Environment, University of Auckland Waipapa Taumata Rau, for facilitating the two-week stay on Niue in November 2022, and to John Puhiatau Pule of Liku.

Letter from Wales

SAM ADAMS

A single private mine excepted, the era that linked South Wales and coal as indelibly as blue scars on pale skin, and possibly for ever, seems over, but it doesn't take much to reactivate memories of Gilfach Goch, when that small, separate nook between the ribbon development of the Rhondda and Ogmore valleys to east and west had three working pits going full pelt. On this occasion the nudge was supplied by a book from Parthian, *Miner's Day* (2021). It is a splendid concept combining the text of B.L. Coombes's Penguin Special *Miners Day* (1945), which is a good deal slimmer not only because the pages are almost tissue-paper thin, wartime paper-rationing standards applying, with an expanded display of work by the artist Isabel Alexander, who contributed half a dozen black-and-white illustrations to that earlier iteration. Alongside a gallery of finely drawn scenes and portraits, the paintings reproduced in this new book, including several of Gilfach, all slag black, grey and muted greens, reveal in its full monstrous glory the industrial vandalism of landscapes that accompanied the creation of Valleys mining communities.

Bertie Louis Coombs Griffiths, the writer's name as it appears in childhood documentary records, has turned up a few times in previous 'letters' because he is a reliable source of information about coal mining, and I mean by that what it was like actually to work underground hacking at black seams a dozen inches to a dozen feet or more thick and loading drams (or 'trams') with coal to be hauled to the surface as fuel for industrial furnaces and ships and to keep home fires burning. The previous references were all from *These Poor Hands* (1939), his more expansive Gollancz Left Book Club autobiography. Alexander's illustrations of miners, pits, terraced housing and gigantic slag heaps, all very familiar to me, were made *in situ*. Although different from the broader, more rural aspect of the upper Neath valley of Coombes's experience, the images are powerfully atmospheric: the combination of writer and artist works.

Peter Wakelin's helpful introduction to the Parthian text tells us a good deal about Coombes, but may leave the reader wanting to know more. How does it come about that someone born in Wolverhampton and brought up in Herefordshire should spend his adulthood in the western anthracite zone of the South Wales coalfield? There's a ready answer to that, for in the second half of the nineteenth century thousands of young men from neighbouring rural counties of England, many with wives and children, were drawn into South Wales in the hope (by no means always or for any length of time realised) of finding regular employment and a decent wage. Then again we might wonder why a writer who published two important and eminently readable autobiographical studies of manual labour in the harshest of environments should divulge so little about his own background and upbringing. It is almost as though life for him began with that journey to the coalfield. I have been attempting to fill the gaps by looking into his family history, so far as the internet allows. In the process I may have stumbled upon a reason for his reticence.

The writer was born in Wolverhampton, 9 January 1893, when his name was registered as Bertie Louis C Griffiths. His mother, Harriet, was the daughter of John Griffiths, a farm labourer, and his wife Elizabeth. The latter was Tompson before marriage, a name worth noting because in the future it would be mentioned by her grandson trying to fill gaps in an ill-recorded family tree. The Griffiths family home was in St Margarets, Herefordshire, some fifty miles from Bertie's birthplace and the surname Harriet declared clearly tells us that she was unmarried at the time of his birth. In 1901, we find her (still Griffiths), with her infant son, much closer to home, employed as housekeeper to Henry Vale, a shoe repairer, and his two grown-up nephews in Hereford. It was only in the autumn of 1902, when she married James Cumbes (the spelling varies) that the 'C' in her son's name was decoded. As things turned out he was their only child. James Cumbes had served in the Boer War 1899–1902 (perhaps the J Coombs who was a sapper in the Royal Monmouthshire Regiment) and carried a limp because some time during the conflict his horse fell and rolled on him. It appears that soon after marrying, like all those others seeking steady work, the couple and their son moved to South Wales. They settled in Treharris, Glamorgan, midway between Pontypridd and Merthyr Tydfil, where (presumably Griffiths) family relations lived and one of the deepest mines of the coalfield, then producing 327,000 tons of coal annually, employed two thousand men. How long they remained in Treharris is uncertain. In any case it was long enough for Bertie to do well at the elementary school he attended – so well, indeed, that he was able to boast later he had passed the examination for admission to a secondary grammar school with the highest marks, 'top of the county' in local parlance. What would have become of him had he taken up the place his success had earned we shall never know because, sick of coal or yearning for the rural life, in 1905/6 James Coombes took wife and son back to Herefordshire where he had acquired the tenancy of Blenheim Farm, Madley.

It was not a propitious move. No matter how much labour was invested in it, there was not enough land to make the farm viable. Bertie, still in his early teens, obtained employment as groom to a local doctor who visited patients in a horse and trap. Though pleasant enough, it could not last. As 'a strong sixteen or nearly seventeen' he set off again for South Wales. This time his destination was Resolven in the upper Neath valley, the western anthracite zone of the coalfield, where there were four collieries which in the century of their existence produced between them almost three million tons of coal. He settled and married there and the few subsequent moves were all in the same still substantially rural locality.

In extracts from a further, unpublished autobiography, *With Dust Still in His Throat*, edited by Bill Jones and Chris Williams (UWP, 1999), Coombes writes of friendships in the mine, bonds of mutual care, and trust and reliance strengthened by daily shared exposure to mortal danger. The experience lasted over forty years, during thirty of which he also served as 'the skilled ambulance man in the colliery', the one called from his usual job at the coal face to deliver first aid. And the calls came frequently: 'I believe I could assess at least one slight injury every day and a more serious one every week. Quite a few hundred journeys to various towns and villages with injured men... Usually in the night also, to disturb some wife or mother from her sleep with the homecoming of a badly injured person... if it was not worse than that.' He recounts one occasion when the 'deputy' responsible for their underground district called him and a workmate to assist in clearing a blocked rail track: 'Ten minutes later I was standing dazed in complete darkness and silence. Each side of me, so close that I could touch either by spreading my elbows, was a huge stone which had fallen without a crack of warning from a height of about eighteen feet. In the darkness I called to the two men who had been with me. Neither could answer. I had seen many smaller accidents but this was the first time death had crashed down against my elbow.'

'A Soul at the "White Heat"'

Poetry, the Author, and the Advent(ure) of Large Language Models

JUDITH BISHOP

I

Was the Death of the Author, announced by Roland Barthes in 1967, an 'accident' of thinking? Like, or unlike, the swipe of the laundry truck that killed the writer one morning in the Quartier Latin – *écrasé*, crushed – a brutal word, close to *erase* – shutting down the body of a singular man who, later in life, had fallen in love with his own human singularity?

'What *did you do*, Ray? Aw, shit...' – Dr Peter Venkman to Dr Raymond Stantz, *Ghostbusters* (1984)

Camera Lucida, Barthes's most poignant work, had appeared in 1980. In 1981, Yves Bonnefoy, whose work exudes a grave vitality very different from Barthes's, was elected to the Chair at the Collège de France left open by the latter's death in 1980. I was first attracted to Bonnefoy's work by a poem about a lizard on a wall. It opens:

> The startled salamander freezes
> And feigns death.
> This is the first step of consciousness among the
>   stones,

and it ends:

> How I love that which gives itself to the stars by the
>   inert
> Mass of its whole body,
> How I love that which awaits the hour of its victory
> And holds its breath and clings to the ground.
> ('Place of the Salamander', translation by Galway
>   Kinnell)

Bonnefoy elaborated a philosophy of 'presence'. He tracked the movement of consciousness as it tries and fails to get a grip on the world: each image a tombstone closing over what it claims to represent. Reading this poem, I, too, freeze – and give my body up to stars – and hold my breath. I can never see a lizard on a wall in a garden without recalling these lines.

Yet it's Barthes, his predecessor, who grips my attention when I think about the advent of large language models (LLMs to those who know).

I notice that *poignant* derives from the French for *to puncture* or *to prick.* The earlier Barthes had decisively skewered the Romantic authorial voice with its source in a singular body: '[W]riting is the destruction of every voice, of every point of origin. Writing is that neutral, composite, oblique space where our subject slips away, the negative where all identity is lost, starting with the very identity of the body writing.' – Roland Barthes, *The Death of the Author.*

But the later Barthes would write: 'The photograph is literally an emanation of the referent. From a real body, which was there, proceed radiations which ultimately touch me, who am here...' (Roland Barthes, *Camera Lucida*). I'm touched both by the insight and the feeling of *having-been-touched* that the author confides to us in this later passage.

Perhaps the Death of the Author hadn't carried away on its plural tide *every* point of origin.

II

Barthes proposes to examine 'the phenomenon of photography in its absolute novelty in world history' (*The Grain of the Voice*). I feel strangely moved by Barthes's perception of this 'absolute novelty': a threshold that is crossed *only once and for all time.*

The unique impression made by light waves rebounding from an object generates a singular set of reflections. The physical impression of a material existence in time (an impression from that moment on detached from the being it reflects) constitutes the 'absolute novelty' which Barthes sought to pierce with his insight, reflecting on the exquisite sensations that 'certain photographs' made in his body and mind.

Human written language also detaches itself from the time and the place in which its meanings were composed by a singular body – thereby sharing a trace or impression of those meanings beyond that time and place.

Language can detach itself from material sources in other ways, too. Many word-randomisers and writing generators have existed over time, making the authorial voice a process of selection and curation from external inputs, underwritten by chance. A predilection for the offerings of chance is evident in centos and was fantasised by Stéphane Mallarmé in his 1897 poem 'Un Coup de Dés' (A Throw of the Dice).

Large language models are statistical machines for generating writing that take these prior interests to another level. Both randomness and likelihood are built into the generation process. Models such as ChatGPT, BLOOM and LaMDA can generate texts in many genres, including summaries, captions, dialogue and verse. Engineers and marketers refer to poetry as one of the genres of creative expression to which large language models will 'democratise' access (perhaps as calculators have 'democratised' maths, by doing the calculations).

But is it poetry?

Google's Verse by Verse engine is an example of that effort. The Google Research website gives anyone access to its large language model, specially trained on the works of 'classical American poets'. It can generate lines according to specifications such as 'quatrain', 'couplet' or 'free verse'. It can produce a consistent number of syllables per line, ranging from 4 to 12 (or else, a random number) and it can tailor its outputs (though imperfectly) to one of four rhyme schemes (in addition to free verse).

The human writer's tasks are these. First, to choose the 'muse' whose style will be mimicked in the output. Second, to initiate the generation process by giving the first line, known as the 'prompt'. Third, to choose the verse type. Fourth, to click the 'generate' button and choose a line from the offered set. And finally, to give the poem its title. To test the process, I composed an example using Emily Dickinson as 'muse'. I asked the program for couplets with eight syllables. Every line below (except the first line and the title) is exactly as provided, in the order generated. The attribution at the end was suggested by the model. Bees came up often in the lines it offered.

The Bee, my Brother

Call to me, my darling brother
White as the snow, as gold as snow.
She bent behind a song to pass,
Every one she sealed alas!
She had a daily drunken bee,
Who falls in rare variety.
She felt as if she held that night
Through centuries to dark, to light.
She had a daily drunken bee,

Who falls in timid honesty.

Written by the user
Inspired by Emily Dickinson

Parodic air aside, you will notice that some of the lines play fast and loose with physical fact ('as gold as snow') and spatial relations ('She bent behind a song'). But we shouldn't be misled. The source of this freedom is not an understanding of metaphor or the flights of a keen poetic licence that, observing the world, has chosen to transform it. Large language models simply lack any grounding in our physical reality. They do not know that snow is white or that a song has no dimensions in physical space. In the verse they make, word and world can never meet.

III
The advent of photography disrupted the reign of painting, and the appearance of writing overturned the oral epic. Certain values and cultural attitudes were lost. But so much was given to us that we never had before. Photography created the possibility of spontaneously recording important events, as they unfold, for posterity. Without writing, we would have none of the novels, stories, plays and books of poetry that we possess today.

So why do I feel rattled?

Perhaps because the large language models outdo all previous methods for engaging chance in the process of writing. They erase the 'body writing' entirely as a 'point of origin' for the production of words. In the space of language models – exchanging 'prompt' for 'thought' in the closing line of Mallarmé's darkly glittering poem – '[e]very prompt projects a throw of the dice'.

And I think: never before have so many words (billions) from so many writers (millions) been scraped from the internet and poured (unaccounted for, deidentified) into the mixing bowl of training data for a set of algorithms.

And never before – given the power of patterns made visible by massive data sets – have the stirrers had such an (un)canny statistical knowledge of the sequences of language, generated by exceptional mathematics and engineering (with a huge, but greatly overlooked, leg-up from linguistics).

So here we are: language as literal grist to the mill of commerce. And another revolution in human expressive technology. Other revolutions have turned out rather well. So is my angst just a personal fear? Would I care if these models hadn't taken aim at poetry, troubling the future of creative expression?

Far more urgent needs do exist for this technology, especially in health (say, translating for refugees when interpreters are scarce, or summarising conversations with your doctor).

Instead, the Death of the Author has taken on a physical form, stamping fear into writers. It's as if we couldn't help but think it into being: the large language model as Stay-Puft Marshmallow Man.

IV
An obvious question might occur to the reader. Won't writers, by editing the outputs of large language models,

create compositions that will, despite their automated source, reflect the writer's purposes, their experience, desires, just as much as before?

Perhaps. And yet, there's more at stake.

I find Barthes's trajectory as a writer from *The Death of the Author* to *Camera Lucida* exceptionally moving at a moment in history when, for the first time, the presence of a human body is no longer essential to generate language.

Maybe that's it.

This technological break is so powerful as to force our admission that a threshold has been crossed. As it was with the invention of photography and the advent of writing.

That's why I want to bear witness to this change. Before the feeling fades.

And no doubt, the astonishment of '*that-has-been*' [in response to the Photograph] will also disappear. It has already disappeared: I am, I don't know why, one of its last witnesses (a witness of the Inactual), and this book is its archaic trace. (Roland Barthes, *Camera Lucida*)

V

I can't help but see a relationship between writing as an animating force, and Barthes's sense of certain photographs as a happening, a piercing and a puncturing of and by the reality of death: 'I wanted to explore it not as a question (a theme) but as a wound: I see, I feel, hence I notice, I observe and I think.'

(Life's animation by death is paradoxically potent.)

This quote turns René Descartes' famous declaration, 'I think, therefore I am', on its head. To be conscious is to feel. And feeling is the ground on which a thinking being stands: 'the condition of an interiority which I believe is identified with my truth' (Roland Barthes, *Camera Lucida*).

I repeat to myself: the 'condition of an interiority which I believe is identified with my truth'. And I think (because I feel): What if human writing emerges from the singularity of a human body (sensory organs, hormones, nervous system, and the whole embodied mind) that has developed, like a photograph, from every impression it receives throughout its growth – all the accidents of life, good and bad – in a process that doesn't end, for as long as those impressions continue to be made upon and held by the body?

And I think (because I feel): What if pleasure and pain are resonances, struck and amplified by each of our encounters with *that* – where *that* may be a word, an idea, a texture or a touch; a face or a name, a gesture or a voice – *that which* – astonishingly, for what are the odds? – is attuned to the complex resonator that developed inside my own singular body? And what if those 'frequencies' could be thought of as the unique signatures of my body in contact with this world – like the knots and the twists and the rings of a tree that has met with strong winds or the interference of other branches in the course of its growth – but also mild conditions that allowed the laying down of sturdy heartwood?

And I hear again: 'The photograph is literally an emanation of the referent. From a real body, which was there, proceed radiations which ultimately touch me, who am here...' (Roland Barthes, *Camera Lucida*).

Responding to this passage, Michael Moriarty writes: 'what is peculiar to photography is the unbreakable coupling of the image to its referent in the real world'.

But the advent of digital manipulation and image generation has broken that 'unbreakable' coupling. This only serves to underline the sheer progress (fundamentally driven by commercial investments) human beings have collectively made towards cutting off language and image from the material earth, including our body, *which was once the only place in which they grew*.

Barthes's words defined photography. But could they extend to writing? Human bodies, too, are marked by emanations from experience. How could our words and meanings touch others if not by mind- and body-piercing sounds, resounding in the grain of all we've lived?

Barthes distinguishes the source of linguistic impressions from the (then) adamantly physical source of photographs on the basis of what he calls certainty: 'No writing can give me this certainty. It is the misfortune (but also perhaps the voluptuous pleasure) of language not to be able to authenticate itself.' And he writes: 'the elaborations of the text, whether fictional or poetic, [are] never credible *down to the root*' (*Camera Lucida;* original emphasis).

Yet, reading back his own words, I wonder, did he not feel certainty? Did those words not bear witness to their source in his singular existence? Certain passages of Barthes's touch me deeply with their gestures and their meanings. These passages speak to some formation in myself, and set it ringing with a strange new animation, however many times I read these words.

They feel credible *down to the root*.

VI

If human language was once imagined as the place where existence speaks through us, who or what speaks in generated writing? 'The place of the real in all this is problematic' as Michael Moriarty says of Barthes's 'Death of the Author' phase.

I think: we have absented ourselves from our common creation, language, as never before in human history. And with that absence, we risk devaluing, even abandoning, the vital connection between language and the real.

VII

Like Bonnefoy in the salamander poem, I love that our consciousness can mediate our access to material reality. Stitching our being and the outside world together, in a rapid shuttling motion, every moment of our lives.

That's why, if you tell me that large language models are writing poetry today, I will tell you: our definitions of poetry differ at the root. The root – contested as it is – that separates machine from human being, and grafted automaton from simple conscious life.

VIII

For Emily Dickinson, the process of writing (both herself and her poems) was imagined as a forge. That forge was lodged in the singular existence she referred to as a *Soul*. She asked a question that still feels audacious now:

'Dare you see a Soul at the "White Heat"?' The poem closes:

> Least Village, boasts its Blacksmith
> Whose Anvil's even ring
> Stands symbol for the finer Forge
> That soundless tugs – within –
>
> Refining these impatient Ores
> With Hammer, and with Blaze
> Until the Designated Light
> Repudiate the Forge –

When I write, I test ideas, words and metaphors against my inner 'anvil' to hear how they ring (right or wrong, sharp or flat). Those 'soundless tugs – within –' are minute judgements that carry with them the subtle gradations and varying intensities of a positive, neutral, or negative feeling – a pleasure or revulsion. It's these that prompt my choices. And at times, the tugs are so intense that it feels as if the brain catches fire with the flames of a metaphoric heaven or hell. Reading and writing can be a gift or gutting.

Dickinson felt this when reading others' books. But I think the same happened when she read her own creations, testing each for its capacity to freeze or burn her soul: 'If I read a book [and] it makes my whole body so cold no fire can ever warm me, I know that is poetry. If I feel physically as if the top of my head were taken off, I know that is poetry. These are the only way I know it. Is there any other way.' Dickinson's 'finer Forge / That soundless tugs – within –' is simulated by the statistical machinations of large language models, which, ranging over trillions of possible sequences of words, select those strings whose frequency of co-occurrence in the training data and aptness of context suggest they can match the semantics of a prompt. Statistical 'weights', then, are the triggers for the choices that they make.

As it stands, language models still require our input. But in future, even the initial instruction or prompt (say, 'write a sonnet on the death of my mother') could be a sequence of words generated by *another* language model. A third model may adjust and refine the written outputs. There needn't be a human here at all.

And yet, I insist, it won't be poetry unless a human being, with their inner forge blazing, is somehow, somewhere, present in the process – having learned with sweat and tears, at the forge of trial and error, 'how to weigh the harvest of light', as the late Australian poet Robert Adamson wrote.

IX

One way to read Emily Dickinson's poems is by passing through the thicket of her variorum of drafts, documented in Sharon Cameron's book *Choosing Not Choosing,* which follows the written traces of those 'soundless tugs – within – / Refining these impatient / Ores'.

For the architects of language models, it's easy to imagine the human writer as a decision-making machine – choosing / not choosing – and human intelligence as a complex, but replicable, sequence of perception, deci-

sion and action.

In this model, human writers might think of possible patterns or distillations of words or ideas (perceiving the contents of their mind). They might then take the time to choose between them, presenting the results of their choices to the reader.

In similar fashion (if you accept the premise), a large language model generates words, chooses the sequence with the strongest rating, and offers that sequence. For language models, writing is indeed nothing more than Barthes's 'neutral, composite, oblique space'.

But lacking a body, and without access to the physical world, language models can neither know nor feel the harm (or the good) their words could do.

X

Barthes wrote: 'the photograph of the missing being, as Sontag says, will touch me like the delayed rays of a star'. Certain poems can do the same.

Barthes referred to his '"ontological" desire' to understand photography and what this technology did that was entirely new to history. I feel the same desire in regard to language models.

In 1882, Nietzsche wrote: 'Lightning and thunder require time; the light of the stars requires time; deeds, though done, still require time to be seen and heard. This deed [the death of God] is still more distant from them than the most distant stars – and yet they have done it themselves.' That delay is why we need to bear witness, even as they unfold, to the impacts of large language models on consciousness, poetry and other language arts. Barthes wrote in *Camera Lucida*: 'What matters to me is not the photograph's "life" (a purely ideological notion) but the certainty that the photographed body touches me with its own rays and not with a superadded light.'

And so I come back to the idea of resonance – the strike of the hammer on our innermost anvil – and the adventure of the writer in their search for human company. The company of those who show us, through a detail or an insight, that we are not alone when we meet in certain poems, as Barthes did in certain photographs, 'the wakening of intractable reality'.

References
Barthes, Roland, *Camera Lucida: Reflections on Photography* (New York: Hill and Wang, 1980)
Barthes, Roland, *The Grain of the Voice* (New York: Hill and Wang, 1985)
Bonnefoy, Yves, *On the Motion and Immobility of Douve.* Translated by Galway Kinnell, with an introduction by Timothy Mathews (Newcastle upon Tyne: Bloodaxe Books, 1992)
Cameron, Sharon, *Choosing Not Choosing: Dickinson's Fascicles* (Chicago and London: University of Chicago Press, 1992)
Google Research. https://sites.research.google/verse-byverse/. Accessed 12 January 2023
Moriarty, Michael, *Roland Barthes* (Cambridge: Polity Press, 1991)
Nietzsche, Friedrich, *The Gay Science*, trans. Walter Kaufmann (New York: Vintage Press, 1974)

Montpeyroux Sonnets

MARILYN HACKER

And once again I wish it were the past
and I were joking with Marie-Geneviève
in her cluttered car... she, still alive,
cat yowling on the back seat, with our dest-
ination, Pénestin, the sea, at last
close by. She'd stretch canvas at night, engrave
draw surreal seas. A double vitrail she gave
me's over my bed, at home.... Where's home? A list
follows, places that were, or felt as if...
Manhattan, north London, Hamra, le Marais ..
If I could go somewhere, where would I go?
Up to the 6th floor of the rue Barrault?
The Tah Marbuta garden? Or just stay
here, fan whirring overhead, one more hot day?

Fan whirring overhead. One more hot day,
dependent on 'devices' with their pass-
words that lock me out. On the terrace,
between two lines of laundry, quickly dry,
a black and white cat stretches, stares at me,
and bolts over the wall, delinquent grace
not quite domesticated. Fixed in place
by heat, I vegetate. Bolt over my
own wall, be... where? The one good restaurant's shut
after disastrous fire. The hairdresser
'fermé pour cause de maladie'. A cat,
a clothesline where old T-shirts dry.
                                        Elsewhere
stays elsewhere, on a map, hovers in air,
shapeshifts on wind, before the wind gets hot.

Shapes shift on wind, before the wind gets hot
and static. Heat hangs like a bad smell
or a headache some unavailable
pill could disperse. I think I'm resolute
remaining unrecumbent, so I sit
under the fan upstairs dispensing cool
air when the sun drops from its canicule
zénith, when it can only circulate
heat. I want to wonder. I want to want
something, someone. There's equilibrium
in hungers, with their surplus energy
refocused: lust to generosity,
 avarice endowing a museum,
gluttony cooking one more ratatouille.

Gluttony, to cook more ratatouille
in this heat. In fact, my stomach's sour.
I sit in the same place another hour
under the spinning fan. I want to be
where? In a body let's say forty-three
years old, taking a stroll in a spring shower,
discussing sex, or politics, or power...
As if! if 'she' were spared 'military
opérations', plague, famine.... I sit on privilege

like a cushion, even if my spine
hurts, mouth is bilious, the dull facts of 'age'
omnipresent. I read what Josephine
Jacobsen wrote late. Sybille Bedford, eighty-nine?
I think of Fairouz last time she went on stage.

I think, was Fairouz, last time she came on stage
(it may have been last week) as plagued with aches
in her articulations? But the breaks
in her voice were art, sorrow and rage –
Beirut, a melody poised at the edge
of keening, longing. She, I, who? awakes
mourning our irrevocable mistakes.
Zakaria Tamer's tiger in a cage
sulked for nine days, then ate what he was fed
the tenth. And the story takes me back
not to this fable or another, but
to 'seasons of translation,' head to head
– some dictionary's hint takes up the slack –
between what might have been, and what was not.

Between what might have been and what was not,
estranging decades. The estranging rain
falls on the street. September's here again.
Umbrellas, Bikes, would knock you down without
stopping (did once, broke my wrist) in fleets, flout
traffic lights, and a pedestrian
fends for herself.
                    My back has made me mean
as watered wine, gluten-free bread. I blot
bleak thoughts out, reading headlines on a screen
here, in the city, up four flights of stairs.
But on the screen, the same cluster of wars
detonates daily. Sunlight, change, change, pain
acedia. A day dumped down the drain
with what was not, although it might have been.

What was not, although it might have been
worse than it was, was still a train-wreck. Why
did I stop going to the bakery,
buying pears, chicken breasts, eating, when
September ripened, spread its ample plen-
itudes? Platitudes! With despair in my
face, up close, every diminishing day,
I locked the door that ought to stay open
to people, possibilities. Those nights
and days a blur. I slept. I bathed. I dressed
and sat there, mind blank, everyone I missed
missing. I was dragged out, and forced
alive, under the vilifying lights,
where once again, I wished it were the past.

*Note: Fairuz is a popular Lebanese singer, about ten years
older than I am, and I think still performing. Zakaria Tamer,
same vintage, is a Syrian writer of very short stories, some-*

times like fables, including the one about the tiger who would not eat in captivity. Marie-Geneviève Havel was a good friend, a painter and engraver from Normandy, who died of non-Hodgkin's lymphoma in 2017 at eighty-six, and in the prime of life. Her work is on the covers of my poem collections Essays on Departure, Alphabets of Sand *and* Blazons.

After Elizabeth Bowen

ANGE MLINKO

They had chemistry. Emmeline had never known chemistry.
Or if she had, it was the night the stemware went over the railing
when a sailor kissed her. That's it. She never anticipated the tears:
glass ellipses, glass dashes, glass exclamation marks
punctuating all tenses, genders, numbers and persons,
each indicating the end of a sentence left unsaid.

But how can you indicate the end of a sentence left unsaid?
I put down the novel. A mole is a measurement in chemistry
– I know that – but J. staring at one on a person's
shoulder said it was like a currant in white icing. They were reeling,
on the stairs, from the sherry and preponderance of remarks
that contrabassed or blunderbussed to a finale of tears.

I pick up the novel again. I welcome the random rips and tears
in the fabric of reality that allow me to glimpse the unsaid
from a distance of a century, or another country, where marks
or pounds or rubles were currency, or chimerae, or chemistry
hadn't been invented yet – though there is obviously the roiling
of the human heart in every age, wherever there are persons

and obstacles, encumbrances, featured in these persons'
lives portend defeat. The reason for Emmeline's tears
was that M. had built up a tolerance to her beauty, riling
her with 'one can't live on top of the Alps' – the unsaid
being either the distillate or what was burnt off in the chemistry
crucible (wasn't she the kind to always get good marks?).

And what about C., the coquette or catalyst who first catches Mark's
eye, then hands Emmeline off to him like oblivious persons
who only notice the effects of their own chemistry?
Hence the lachrymal ellipsis where the sentence tears
itself off because it cannot bear to end except in the unsaid.
And the one currant on the cupcake of a shoulder that is rolling

backward into the past, from a London party overruling
all that had come before, begs the question: what marks
a life if not a bad bargain? Couldn't he have unsaid
'You expected too much' –? It wasn't as if several persons
from his past didn't warn her. It wasn't as if her tears
could soften him like acid rain on marble in chemistry.

(Marble, my darling, is soft as rocks go.) Chemistry, tears,
persons: she (I) asked him (you) to turn off the light…. The railing
marks precisely where the car trailed off like an apology ____

 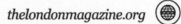

The Con of the Wild

SILIS MACLEOD

'Deep in the forest a call was sounding, and as often as he heard this call, mysteriously thrilling and luring, he felt compelled to turn his back upon the fire and the beaten earth around it, and to plunge into the forest, and on and on, he knew not where or why; nor did he wonder where or why, the call sounding imperiously, deep in the forest.' – Jack London, *The Call of the Wild*

Often called 'Europe's Last Great Wilderness', Highland Scotland holds great emotive power for those who know it well as much as for those who do not. We have a strong impression of the place: its mountains, lochs, coasts, the bothies. One of the most iconic images of the Highlands must be that postcard scene of a sloping hillside above a sea loch, on which is perched a small, whitewashed cottage with a red tin roof, seen from behind as if approaching home. It conjures the twin (mutually exclusive) emotions of wilderness and domesticity. 'Golly', the spirit says, 'isn't that a wild and desolate place', adding: 'Wouldn't it be something to live there, in that wee house'. (Or, more probably, to go on holiday there for a bit.)

Everything is wild these days. If you need to buy something to do with gardening, the natural world or the outdoors, chances are that the company selling it will be a Wild*this* or Wild*that*. Just search for a local florist on Google and the results will confirm the spread of the contagion. But flowers, grown in captivity – that is on a flower farm, usually in monocultural fields in the Netherlands – are not wild. They are the bloom of wilderness's opposite: cultivation. Cut flowers are the colourful semaphore of our enduring and successful domesticity in what was once a hostile environment. Yet, due to the extent of our divorce from that environment, the thing now is to *reconnect* with nature. To go out and be amongst it, to *bathe* in it. The wilder the better. And why? To recharge our depleted batteries. And if you can't go out and be amongst it, order the wild in. Go online and get some delivered to your door, or through a friend's letterbox (see Bloom & Wild).

Scotland is the recipient of more than its fair share of such wilderlust. In 2014, the BBC reported that 19.5 percent of Scotland was wilderness (an impressively precise figure for a landscape said to be 'wild' or unquantifiable). The usual northern spaces were commended by Scottish Natural Heritage (SNH): Wester Ross, Sutherland and Knoydart. Clearly Ian Jardine, SNH's chief exec, has never visited Glasgow's Parkhead neighbourhood on the morning of an Orange March. Representatives from the John Muir Trust and Ramblers Scotland appraised the wild areas as 'assets' supporting 'sustainable economic growth'. The BBC's accompanying photography raised the call of the wild with dramatic images of the Cairngorms (a spruce plantation stretching down to a lochside), a hill in Wester Ross (managed as a grouse moor) and an undisclosed sea loch (in which there is the distinct black circle of a fish farm cage).

These are certainly 'assets', but are they in any meaningful sense wild?

Writing on the strange vocabulary of 'wilderness' and 'wilderness preserves' in America, Wendell Berry argues:

> The so-called wilderness, from which we purposely exclude our workaday lives, is in fact a place of domestic order. It is inhabited, still, mainly by diverse communities of locally adapted creatures living, to an extent always limited, in competition with one another, but within a larger, ultimately mysterious order of interdependence and even cooperation... The wildest creatures to be found in any forest, if not surface miners and industrial loggers, are the industrial vacationers with their cars, cameras, computers, high-tech camping gear, and other disturbers of domestic tranquility and distracters of attention.

Wilderness is a place of homes, domus more discrete, complex and subtle than the grids of the city or the green lawns of suburbia.

Northern Scotland features so heavily in our collective doting on the wild because it is a depopulated landscape. But a depopulated landscape is not the same as a wild one. Places so often lauded as 'wild' – Sutherland, Wester Ross, Knoydart – were once peopled and full of human industriousness. The sheltered glens, now home to blackface sheep and red deer stags, were the reserve of crofting families, raising lives (human and animal) and subsisting from the albeit poor soil around them. Now we look to these largely deforested areas teeming with bracken and we shudder. The piles of granite rubble which once formed people's homesteads are today less impressive than the stone dykes between sheep fields. We feel the rain and hear the squelch of our boots in the acidic mud as we walk by. *It must have been a hard life out here!*

*

The tourist sign at Badbea Clearance Village, in southern Caithness, refers to the landowner Sir John Sinclair, owner of the Langwell Estate, as an 'agricultural improver'. Such 'improvements' included the letting of vast swathes of his estate to wealthy Lowland farmers running Cheviot sheep at hugely increased rents. To facilitate this, existing tenant crofting families had to be evicted. They were forcibly moved to harsh coastal areas, such as Badbea, where high winds meant they had to tether their livestock and children to the hillside. When agricultural life proved too difficult here, they were encouraged to join the booming herring fishing industry. As a race of inland subsistence farmers, the crofters had little knack for seagoing. Many perished at sea. In 1790, the same Sir John Sinclair, also an authority on statistical analysis, pondered how one might analyse the 'quantum of happiness' in Scotland.

On the northwest coast, difficult to reach, accessible only by foot or small ferry, Knoydart is usually toted as one of the wildest areas of Europe. To which the 'Men of Knoydart', in the traditional folksong reply:

It was down by the farm of Scottas Lord Brocket walked one day
When he saw a sight that troubled him far more than he could say
For the seven men of Knoydart were doing what they planned
They'd staked their claims, they were digging drains on Brocket's private land [...]
Then up spoke the men of Knoydart, You have no earthly right
For this is the land of Scotland and not the Isle of Wight
When Scotland's proud Fianna wi' ten thousand lads is manned
We'll show the world that Highlanders have a right tae Scottish land

Here, on a remote peninsula, seven crofters staked their claim to the land by digging drains and improving it. It is not until such men (and women) are removed from the picture that we can begin to think of this landscape as in any sense 'wild', as we use the word today.

Elsewhere, in South Uist, the introduction of the wild followed familiar lines. This, from *Scottish Island Hopping: A Guide for the Independent Traveller* (1994):

Colonel John Gordon of Cluny, who bought the island in 1838, got a government relocation grant to clear the land for sheep. His most infamous action was to call the people to a public meeting, threatening a fine for non-attendance. Once there, police, bailiffs and press gangs seized many from the crowd and put them on the *Admiral*, a ship anchored in Lochboisdale and bound for Canada. Resisters were clubbed and dragged aboard, in what was compared to a slave hunt on the African coast. Around 1,000 people left the island on that ship, many of them to destitution in Toronto and Hamilton. The population, 2,200, is now a third of what it was then.

South Uist is home to RSPB Loch Druidibeg, where visitors are invited to 'Take a walk on the wild side' in an 'excellent example of Uist moorland and loch... We [RSPB] are managing the area [as the crofters once did] to benefit the diverse range of wildlife from carnivorous plants to the mighty sea eagle.'

Today, it is the sheep that are being cleared. Government agencies such as DEFRA and the Scottish Land Commission want fewer sheep on the upland hillsides of the United Kingdom. These areas should now deliver alternative methods of 'sustainable growth'. Whether it be habitat creation, carbon capture opportunity (in the form of new plantations and sometimes native woodland) or renewable energy generation. Once again, it is the upland, the highland and the rough land that represents the new agri-economic frontier. The muddy gateway to a new eco goldrush.

*

Last year, my erstwhile place of work was invited to participate in a carbon audit of the company's operations. We were asked to consider things such as our place of work, our method of work and the functioning of the company's product in the wider economic environment. 'The company' was a public library, its 'product' was deemed to be 'the book' (I had thought 'literacy' our product *par excellence*). The company which undertook the audit produced its report with one general recommendation: move all reading experiences from print to digital to mitigate 'how much carbon was emitted due to the printing, production, distribution and storage of books'. As librarians, we were castigated as net emitters and were encouraged to invest in carbon offsetting. When I was asked to lead the taskforce to implement the carbon audit report's findings, I politely declined, took my long overdue retirement instead and returned to the isle of Harris.

Despite the historic depopulation across the Highlands, people still live here. I was born here, to a crofting family, which had been gradually moved to the coastline of Harris from the island's comparatively hospitable centre. My family lived and worked the land here. My father had a second job as a carpenter, my mother as productive gardener, both for the nearby estate. They knew the local landscape deeply. As far as Harris had a wilderness, my parents were part of it. Their home, nestled where the heather moor met the rocky shoreline, was a home among other homes. Sea eagles fished in the bay in front and hares leapt from the garden as we stepped out. Otters, seals and whales were daily visitors. This was and still is not an unusual Highland life. Some households dotted across the hill and coast, in Harris and further away, still make a living in this way, much as the traditional crofter did. But another change is underway. A strong wind blows from the south, ushering in a new vocabulary of rewilding, carbon sequestration and 'lost forests'. And a new world of unpeopled landscapes.

In 2020/21, the multinational brewery BrewDog purchased the Kinrara Estate, a 9,000-hectare Highland sporting estate. This hip brewery with a punk ethos became the latest in a line of companies hoping to bury their dirty, emitting production in the Scottish landscape. In winding up the sporting estate, they pledge to regenerate Scotland's forests and, of course, to offset their own carbon footprint. Millions of trees will be planted, they have plans for an ecohotel (whatever that is), a new distillery and an outdoor centre (a wonderful oxymoron!). 'We want the Lost Forest to enable people to reconnect with nature and by doing so become far more cognisant of the impact that we, as humans, are having on our planet', says James Watt, chief exec of BrewDog. As the infrastructure of the sporting estate is dismantled, the few people that did live on the land (gamekeepers, gardeners, estate farmers) are removed. Their houses are sold off, more often than not as holiday homes.

Brewdog's emphasis is on educating the public, showing them around an eco-theme park, everyone assuaging themselves of their collective environmental guilt, then packing the tourists off back to the city. Heaven forbid that anyone make their home, never mind their living, here. As I wrote to my library superior at the time of my resignation: 'Carbon offsetting is a scam – one of the great green-gold rushes of our time – which seeks to divorce the Scottish people from the land once again.'

*

If you need a wilderness, for whatever reason, but cannot get to northern Scotland, why not make your own? This is the vogue of landscape architecture today: rewilding. Knepp Estate, the historic seat of some such ancient English family in rural Suffolk, are the ones responsible for propagating the English variant of what was really a controversial Dutch fringe movement. ('Rewilding Pioneers' is how they would like us to see them.) On finding their vast dairy enterprise didn't turn enough profit, they closed the whole thing down and emptied the barns of all those high-maintenance French coos. Instead, Knepp wanted to fill its acreage with free-roaming herbivores, the mammalian vestiges of a pre-agricultural heyday. According to their website, I believe they still sell meat, but this is not farming, this is wilderness*ing*. The product at Knepp is a hybrid between Michael Crichton's Isla Nublar and a very middle-class Butlins.

It's never long before talk of wilderness brings one back to Scotland again, and so it's no surprise that Knepp has a host of copycat operations here. Bamff Wildland, in northern Perthshire, removed what was a successful organic tenant farming operation, in an area of the country not replete with organic systems, and replaced it with a Scottish Knepp model. And earlier this year the company Highlands Rewilding purchased the 3,500-acre Tayvallich Estate in Argyll for a crowd-funded £10.5 million. The company positions itself as a safeguarder of habitats, whilst 'continuing to target "financial institutions", and also the "affluent rewilding enthusiasts, family offices, foundations, trusts and forward-looking companies" that have already invested £7.6 million.' Tayvallich is a special place, but it's really a patchwork of Scottish west coast farmland with a lot of coastline. 'Affluent rewilding enthusiasts' do not, I'd imagine, care much about the people that have made their living on the estate, farming, fishing and working

their whole life. They will be the first to go under Highlands Rewilding's 'natural-capital verification science', as they term it.

Doing the opposite of traditional farming – rewilding, carbon offsetting, reforestation – is big business these days. The new landowners who are implementing these often government-backed schemes have been termed 'Green Lairds'. And, like the lairds of old, their actions are effecting a second wave of clearances across the whole of rural Scotland. An acre of poor hill land that five years ago sold for between £1,000 and £2,000 changes hands now for figures closer to £10,000 per acre. (The value of productive land is far in excess of this figure.) This makes the likelihood of anyone wanting to purchase and turn an honest living from the land for themselves, their family and the local community an impossibility. And it affects everything in the vicinity too. Land prices affect the cost of housing plots which, in turn, increase the value of rural housing. Young people who grow up in rural areas are priced out and forced to move to apartments in cities and towns. The houses they could have filled with their joyous noise go to the more affluent and sedate generations as holiday homes. And the impression of the Scottish wilderness continues.

But northern Scotland is not a wild place; it is my home. In my nearly eighty years living and travelling in the country I have not witnessed anything that I would call true wilderness. There are some pockets of intense beauty, but the hand of man is never out of sight. A country that abuses its peasantry, abuses the very land itself. As I look across its patchwork of spruce plantations, grouse moors, intensive arable (in the east) and extensive dairy (in the south west), Scotland seems more of a land abused. Our sense of Scotland as a wilderness is predicated on the land uses and abuses of the eighteenth and nineteenth centuries; their emptied glens are our wild spaces. All current projections of the so-called wilderness of Scotland are continuations of the same cultural project that culminated in the violences of the Clearances.

As I look out my window, across hill and coast, I see we are not in balance. The essential relationship between mankind and the world around us has been neglected. And the new green schemes do nothing to right this unbalance. In Scotland, the wilderness we talk about is an invention, a state we have created to ease our troubled souls. As Wendell Berry has said, it is us who are the wild ones – those of us who refuse to live in cooperation with nature, who seek to dichotomise, monetise and digitise its depths, those of us who can use the term 'natural capital' without a deep sense of unease. Scotland is not 'Europe's Last Great Wilderness', but perhaps with the reintroduction of the beaver, the lynx and the wolf on the cards for its future, could it be?

Tribute Paid to the Immortality of the 'Bar Internacional'

CÉSAR TIEMPO

translated by J. Kates and Stephen A. Sadow

When he breaks his vow of solitude
– a poor wedding gift like his daily bread –
the poet lets himself be won over by the city
and by the seven streets of their seven joys.
In front of his door the rural caravan
of Lacroze streetcars passes like a sweet wind
– green gust that unifies the peoples of Israel
Into a bundle of blond souls and rapid dreams –
He climbs aboard and crosses odd numbered avenues
as old as Aion and like Aion modern
and at the noisy curve of Pasteur Street and Corrientes
he enters the bar of bars.
'Bar Internacional!'
where the Jewish clan
innocuously recovers
from the persecutions of Imperial Russia!

One of those Cossacks
– the executioners
who fan the storm – stoops
(from two meters to one-fifty)
in the doorway for two pesos
and folds himself into a ninety-degree angle
with the elasticity of a contortionist
before the good-humored Jews
who can relax at a sight without threat
and forget the crack of knouts
and the servility of hooligans
facing the stage where seven or eight scoundrels
dance and sing and make balalaikas moan.

Surely, they are not Essenes
These insatiable sybarites
who speak in the nasal voice of our forebears
(who say we are, of course, so-called Jews)
while they may add biscotti, sweets, crumpets
to hot teacups, dumplings
they jumble the names of stars, nettles and roses
and look obliquely
with the gaze of a skilled wine-taster
(like butchers who appraise cattle)
The tables are overflowing with lower middle classes
and doctors, doctors, doctors.

Ah, if they were to find a good catch
for their falconer daughters
who look for husbands at Ezra dances
while in the Hebraica Center are the awkward
   prospects
who would let themselves be whipped without crying,
   servile,
beaten down in the synagogues, and, happy,
they chant with trembling lips

the *alh het sheheitano lefoneha* and more!

When the poet comes down to earth, that is to say,
when he stands alone before reality
distant as it is, she who taught him to laugh
launches into a wheedling telephone call
to Samuel Eichelbaum, my dear friend,
sharp as a saber
heartfelt as his theater pieces
filled with fervor and life:
– 'I'm puttin' off the Ritz, and I'm on my way.'
he assures her over the line.
And in the bar, he spins
pinwheels of bitter destiny
and is drenched in his own laughter,
a laughter of stone and whirlwind.

The young night owls
camp out with stubborn happiness
and feed the fire of scandal
while old folks think about their dateless daughters
and Lovya's nose, bulging like
those gourds displayed on the bar
sniffs the neighborhood and his gnome-like eyes
carefully guard what he gives and receives.

(Through thick tortoiseshell glasses
some clients specify smiles and damages
The damages – of course – for the young fathers
and the smiles for Paley's daughters.)

Just before midnight
Don Alberto Gerchunoff
that master of elegant prose
enters as if into town hall.
Fat as a dictionary
and wise in the art of cooking
his ecclesiastical figure dominates
that narrow scene
for his wide-ranging skills
fitting for a rabbi or a man of the church:
he uses parrhesia like a scalpel
and speaks with the same grand music of his prose,
a little woodwind and a little contrabass,
mastering the score he conducts with pleasure,
like his own menu of entertainment,
but this is the melodrama of peace and work
and *mane, shekel, phares* is not his prayer.

The men of the orchestra have already changed
their Cossack costumes for civilian ones;
the lights turned down, the barman balances his
   books:

yawns, smoke, sleep: the party is over.

Tomorrow once again: music, laughter, noise
– it is Saturday, and we sin (Exodus, twenty, ten)
But if you have something you want forgotten
when God is not looking, let's come back again.

The poet has left
and the narrator after him:
   Louche night: three a.m.

César Tiempo (1906–1980) was one of the important Argentine writers of his time as poet, playwright, screenwriter and journalist. Born Israel Zeitlin in Ukraine, and brought to Buenos Aires as an infant, he was a member of the working-class Boedo Writers Group, won the Municipal Prize for Poetry in 1930, the Municipal Prize for Best Screenplay in 1945, and between 1973 and 1975 served as director of the Cervantes National Theatre. *Libro para la pausa del sábado, Sabatión argentino,* and *Sabadomingo* are his best-known books of poetry.

It proved impossible to find the heirs for César Tiempo. His wife and three children are all dead. All of his publishers are long out of business. The publisher of the collection in which I found this poem published only that book, then disappeared.

James Kates writes: Friends since high school days in the early 1960s, Steve and I began translating together while he was a graduate student with a concentration in Latin American Jewish literature. He got to know a dynamic Argentine poet, novelist, and – more recently – a writer of nonfiction autobiography, Ricardo Feier-stein. I read no Spanish at the time, but was fluent in French, comfortable in Latin, and acquainted with Italian. In 1989, we published our first Feierstein selection, *We, the Generation in the Wilderness*. Steve's growing reputation in his field led to other projects, first working with the Peruvian poet Isaac Goldemberg, then into a wide-ranging anthology, *A Voice Among the Multitudes: Jewish Poets from Latin America* (published online by the Northeastern University Press). Next year, we will have another anthology coming out with the University of New Mexico Press, *I Am of the Tribe of Judah: Poems from Jewish Latin America*.

Everything I know about Latin American Jewish poetry I have learned from Steve. He brings a text in Spanish with a rough English draft. By this time, I am confident reading past this draft into the original language, while Steve is familiar enough to have anticipated a lot of my poetic questions, so our process has become more efficient than when we started.

We struggle most with regional particularities of Latin American Spanish, and we have sometimes been led astray in misunderstandings before we caught ourselves in correction. The lines 'Mientras suman cual sondas, dulces, pingüinadosas / en los cálidos pozos de té las quesadillas' gave us a great deal of difficulty, but we generalized it slightly for an international readership into 'while they may add biscotti, sweets, crumpets / to hot teacups, dumplings'. Steve is also especially sensitive to cabalistic undertones and overtones in many of the texts we work with, while I try to be alert to historical references and associations. We talk these out between us before we determine how much will make it overtly into the final English text.

Reviewing Ho! Ho! Ho!

HORATIO MORPURGO

2016: Year of Sticking It to Teacher. Teacher had, it turned out, not been paying enough attention to just over half the class. Jimmy Gay's memoir, *Ho! Ho! Ho! A Poaching We Will Go!* (2017) is in its way the best guide I know to what happened that year and is far from over now. Everything from the cheeky self-published format to its swaggering tone gives voice to the trouble we are in, better than a well-meaning treatise ever could.

*

Some background. After the Second World War, the Canadian Government, seeking to increase revenue from its cod fishery, adopted a new management regime. To maximise yield and eliminate fluctuations in the catch, larger vessels began to fish further offshore all year round. The old seasonal inshore fishery, already in trouble, was dismantled. The changes were felt as far off as Bridport, Dorset, for centuries a supplier of fishing gear to the region. Nine-tenths of the cod-lines in use off Nova Scotia were still in the 1950s manufactured in the town. With larger boats now requiring larger nets, its factories struggled to adapt. One of them, for example, bought a special braiding machine for salmon nets. At one point it was working twenty-four hours a day just to fulfil orders from North America. Remember that: salmon nets.

As continental economies recovered from the war, Bridport's large, older factories fell idle during the 1960s. The loss of imperial markets, advances in automation elsewhere and the introduction of synthetic fibres had already undermined their position. Net-makers continued – and continue – to operate from smaller sites in and around the town. The main ones are Portuguese- and German-owned. One former factory designs products for manufacture in Sri Lanka – owned by a multinational, it operates mainly as a defence contractor. The numbers employed are significant but much reduced. After at least seven centuries the industry is no longer the mainstay of Bridport's economy.

One consequence of this never received the attention it might have. I said to remember those salmon nets because there emerged in the town, during the 1970s and 1980s, organised gangs of salmon poachers known as the 'Bridport Boys', among whom Jimmy Gay was a significant figure. These ranged as far afield as Scotland and Wales but concentrated their operations in the South West of England.

Gay wrote his memoir after suffering a stroke. He hawked it around pubs, angling shops, booksellers and newsagents and died two years after its publication. He'd gone by the time I heard about it from a friend and even then I didn't read it straight away. It's not your standard environmentalist fare. There's nothing hushed or confessional about the story of how he became the 'most wanted on the West country salmon poacher list'. He protests, perhaps too much, that he is not ashamed and would do it all again. On the cover he wears shades and leans back, shirtless, on the bonnet of a gold Jaguar.

The book opens with four photographs of his tattoos – there are leaping salmon with an otter and a barn owl on either flank. Here is a post-modern brave, proud indigene, wrapped in images of natural abundance. From a town built over centuries, through its net-making, on the exploitation of that abundance. Opposite these images are two black-and-white photos, one showing a 38 lb fish taken from a Dorset river, hanging by its tail in his workshop. Another shows a 'good hit' of fish – twenty-five salmon laid out on the concrete floor of a garage.

The first thing that struck me about this imagery was its familiarity. Absent the shades and the Jaguar and he might have been a walking advertisement for the Devon Wildlife Trust. That science teacher looms benign in my own West Country childhood who once walked us across fields to the Tavy. Silenced by a weir's thundering, we stood in the rain on the bank of a river which had been until then little more than the school boundary. Now silver strangers back from the Arctic launched from its tumbling froth or fell back, or insisted and slithered and thrashed their way furiously to the top. I came nose to nose with my first otter late one summer night, on holiday, wading with a torch across another Devon river. Or I'd arrive at the derelict farmhouse half an hour before sunset to wait in the overgrown garden for its resident barn owls to emerge.

The same creature-constellation shed its influence over our very different lives.

*

Enable autocomplete then type 'the boyhood' into Google. Millais's *The Boyhood of Raleigh* is the first prompt which appears below, one hundred and fifty years after the painting was first exhibited. Its title notwithstanding, click on images and it is two boys which appear, infinitely repeated and identically paying attention to an old sailor as he gestures toward the horizon.

The work was an immediate success with the London public. Those who would see here affirmed some peculiarly English call to a destiny beyond European shores should be aware that the old sailor's costume is Genoese. He is shown as being from the Italian Republic which gave birth to Christopher Columbus, as indeed to Giovanni Caboto / John Cabot ('English' discoverer of Newfoundland). Genoa it was also that supplied credit to the Spanish crown as its armies overran Central and South America.

Millais travelled to Budleigh Salterton in 1870. For the sailor he hired a professional model. The two young brothers, Walter and Carew, in elaborate costumes, were the artist's own sons, George and Everett. It's true Walter was born in a farmhouse up the road, but unlikely that he or his brother would at that age have dressed up quite so gaudily to follow a footpath down to the beach.

Such criticisms are of course entirely beside the point. The scene is mythical and the myth, if Google is any guide, remains active. Stand on Chesil Beach, a little to the east of here, looking straight out to sea. If you could plot the direction of your gaze on a map, it would travel 4,000 miles without landfall before crossing the coast of South America. There are mornings when Lyme Bay looks so vast you can almost see its coastline dropping that perpendicular to Brazil, the way you might drop a line to someone you are rather proud of knowing.

Perhaps some local was boasting of this grand connection (I've done it myself) and Millais heard it and it gave him the idea. Such a connection, though, means different things at different times and his painting ties it to a very specific history. Captured here on canvas is the moment that will one day give rise to Raleigh's search for El Dorado. Prefigured here, compressed into that gesture, is the fateful sweep of England's early engagement with the Americas, north and south.

Observe more closely though and anyone who knows the place cannot help asking: why did Millais need to visit Devon at all for this? Its title only suggests a locality if you happen to know where Raleigh grew up. Far more striking than the minimal references to Budleigh Salterton is the near-complete absence from this image of anything recognisable as 'place'. Maybe that's why the cyberpeople like it so much. But Millais could surely have found a stretch of wall and dressed up his sons and a model somewhere closer to home.

The present-day town makes much of this Victorian icon and even recently hosted an exhibition devoted to it. But the desiccated starfish and bit of seaweed are standard beach-scene props, as is the toy boat. We could be anywhere at the edge of any ocean. The costumes give you more or less a European location but the sailor manifestly isn't talking about wherever it is they are – quite the contrary – he is describing something or somewhere well out of sight.

The sea for its part figures largely but this isn't Lyme Bay or anywhere else in particular. This is sea as anonymous means to the end of elsewhere. Water here, in full agreement with the Genoese sailor, gestures over the horizon to where fortunes are made, exotica met with, heroic destinies forged. Elsewhere is represented by a stuffed toucan, a bird which still today charms visitors to South America and figured prominently in the writings of Brazil's earliest European explorers.

The boys' immediate surroundings, in other words, are wired directly into the beyond, into the dawning of a new transcontinental order. The sixteenth century and the West Country together certainly played their part in the establishment of that order, so it's understandable if Millais travelled down to pick up on any lingering vibrations from long ago. I still think there are other ways into this.

*

Ho! Ho! Ho! is mostly made up of short episodes, vignettes. The tone is puckish. Think *Only Fools and Horses*. Here is Gay setting nets in a river on Dartmoor when a coach full of elderly tourists gets stuck on an old stone bridge nearby, from which his activities in the water below are plainly visible. You don't have to be enthusiastic about salmon poaching to find it funny. As with the television series, some episodes hit on a surprising seriousness. That staring coach-load is as fine an image as you will find of collapsing manufacture cheek by jowl with tourism peddling the 'scenic' South West.

Not satisfied with recounting exploits, *Ho! Ho! Ho!* dares to dream, too, of a new generation that will take up the torch. Those who would follow in the trail its author has blazed receive advice, for example, on how to make their own nets, adapting them to particular rivers, setting them to best effect. Many variations on his No Regrets theme are played.

Gay is a self-conscious rebel from the first page, yet he also identifies strongly with a home town in which net-making had been carried on for centuries. Through this guidance on how to make a net, there glimmers unmistakable pride in what 'anyone can do' where he is from. Official Bridport makes much of its net-making past but its post-industrial poaching gangs are never invited to celebrations of this heritage. They are viewed – in so far as their memory has not been conveniently mislaid – as an aberration.

They saw themselves, to judge by *Ho! Ho! Ho!*, as carefree outlaws. As deregulation's Del Boys, they steal cars here, petrol there, dinghies from a campsite. They empty a vicar's fridge. *Trainspotting* meets *Life on Earth* when they hit a deer on the road one night and bundle the injured animal, still alive, into the back-seat, to butcher it later. They stop and catch a fox cub to take home for the kids. They try to steal a foal off Dartmoor, leaving off only when the mother starts trying to demolish their car. You can almost see them back in The Nag's Head, rattling these off as so many merry adventures encountered while in pursuit of fantastical profits.

*

Raleigh did not hear about El Dorado from an imaginary Genoese on the beach at Budleigh. He heard about it from someone he actually met, Pedro Sarmiento, a Spanish nobleman captured during an expedition to the Azores. But who cares where or from whom he heard it?

Neither version explains how a man of such intelligence ever fell for a story like that.

But what if the answer to this lies closer to home? True, Alejo Garcia's expedition had already long ago set out from what is now Argentina, in search of the White King, Lord of the Silver Mountain. It returned without Garcia but with several chunks of silver ore from the region of Potosi. There were precedents, as if the treasures of Cortes and Pizarro were not enough. And Raleigh was doubtless subject to the alchemical fever of his day, with its restless searching after the Universal Panacea.

Raleigh is thought to have known little about mining, though as Lord Warden of the Stannaries he oversaw tin mining in Devon and Cornwall. He is said to have relied for advice in this role on his half-brother Adrian Gilbert, MP for Bridport, who also owned and ran a silver mine in North Devon.

But he knew much more about it than historians credit him with and more than his half-brother could tell him. Raleigh was also Lord Lieutenant for Cornwall, in which role William Carnsewe was a trusted informant. Carnsewe's correspondence has preserved the most vivid account that has survived of conditions down a Cornish mine at this time. Dated to 1584, so two years before the meeting with Sarmiento, the letters reveal a world of fraying tempers and shambolic finances, low-grade ore, round-the-clock work schedules, hastily installed pumps to deal with rainwater or underground springs. Do not read them by candlelight in an enclosed space.

These exasperated reports would certainly have reached Raleigh, who as an MP spoke out on miners' pay. They give us the low-down on strained labour relations and dismal returns at Treworthie. They give us the money troubles and the splashing around in the pitch dark of an actually existing mine in a real place. Imaginative power was at this point his most cunning enemy. This is how the disastrous fairy tale of El Dorado took hold. Sarmiento had only to say the word. A New World city where the king walked down to a lake each morning to wash off all that troublesome gold dust. Such a city would indeed solve everything. How could it not be true?

*

Ted Hughes sat in our front room one Christmas improvising a poem each for my brother and me. He wrote them out on the inside cover of a poem he'd printed off as a pamphlet, all profits to the Atlantic Salmon Trust. I was lucky with teachers. As the ecologist of the family, my dedication begins: 'The fox is in the chicken coop – / The Fleet cleans up the entire shoal. / The Poacher dreams of a jackpot scoop – / "Boom Today – Tomorrow Dole!"'

Poacher, farmer, corporate CEO, government minister: the poem offers each of them a line or two to explain themselves, to offer their excuses for behaving as they do. Gay was indeed on the dole when he took to salmon poaching – it almost makes me wonder now whether Hughes knew of his story. They fished the same rivers. In any case they are all – from poacher to government minister – represented in the poem as responsible for building and operating the machine that is driving salmon to extinction. Yet of all these only the poacher is punished. Himself from a small town in post-industrial Yorkshire, Hughes would have spotted the contradiction. The poacher here is not worse than his more respectable accomplices, just poorer.

To update what was implied but not spelt out in that dedication: it isn't and never was the likes of Jimmy Gay who own dairy farms or shares in BP or book the regular flights. Gay recalls, by contrast, the £38 he was earning for a six-day week in a butcher's shop. He had small children and was 'fed up with always being skint'. He went on the dole which paid the same 'but boy I was bored'.

There immediately follows the book's crucial passage. Together with an experienced poacher, our novice is dropped in a gateway above the river Dart, just where it flows past Dartington College. It is dusk. 'I could see it shine in what light there was left. A lot bigger than the river at home, I thought... we walked down to the river, sacks on our backs. I was already in love with this job.'

Read this passage carefully and what he actually falls 'in love with' is an atmosphere familiar to anyone who has ever walked over fields at dusk, in summer, down to a Devon river. Ask any birdwatcher, any angler. A Victorian entomologist even coined a special word for it: he called it 'dusking'. Gay's argument has no sooner reached this point, however, than it veers sharp right. This first outing to the Dart earns him £50 and suddenly the decision is represented as purely economic. We hear no more of 'boy I was bored'.

In the space of a few pages, the Eighties burst upon the small-town scene in which *Ho! Ho! Ho!* begins. Gay starts wise-cracking as cynically as any City trader. He is suddenly running two Jaguars, removing 550lb of fish from a river in two hours and earning £10,000 a month. The reader has no way of checking these figures but that's not the point: they are presented as a guide to *motives*.

It's doubly ironic that the book's crucial transformation occurs in the grounds of Dartington, at that time a radical and influential art college. Experiments in agriculture and other rural industries, the early music movement and modernist architecture all found a welcome there. Might he, with the right teachers, not have been persuaded to hold on a little longer to that 'boy was I bored' *before* arriving at 550lb of dead wild salmon as the solution?

Why, in fact, was he bored?

Gay takes it as read that no explanation is required. Domestic cares, bills: the long littleness of life already taking over. They are fortunate indeed who do not know that feeling. But the proximity of Dartington College is ironic not only because there were, it appears, no students or staff around to pay attention to what was happening on their doorstep.

It would have taken a prodigiously gifted and a brave teacher, too, to get through to Gay at this point but the teacher I have in mind grew up in Dorset and never forgot it. They'd have had that much in common. Surely there was someone on the premises at Dartington that evening who could have told Gay who John Cowper

Powys was and what he had to say about fish. It might have been worth a try anyway.

At the centre of Powys's *The Art of Happiness* is the image of a leaping fish. He argued that the mind can make friends with more than we are, now, in the habit of imagining. If we have in the past tended to overstate the mind's powers, by contrast we now habitually underestimate them, with devastating consequences. Gay's boredom would have been, for Powys, a symptom which, in one form or another, afflicts all of modern humankind. He thought we generally employ against it one or other of two dodges.

'On the one hand we can pursue what is popularly called 'pleasure', grossly, heedlessly, selfishly, at the expense of all finer considerations. On the other hand we can let our personal life go and give ourselves up to some absorbing Cause which becomes more to us than soul or body.'

We ceaselessly and dishonestly, all of us, proclaim the all-sufficiency of the choice we make. So Gay, for example, premises his book with 'Would I do it again? Bloody right, every last minute!' although there would, of course, by now be rather fewer fish to 'do it again' to. Powys's point is that in accepting this 'choice' as the only one available we betray something essential in ourselves.

What exactly was it that Gay saw in that glimmering of the River Dart at dusk? For Powys, the leaping fish, or 'Ichthean' act, is a primordial third option which modern life seeks to prescribe, for which it has deprived us of even a language we might use for it. 'A fierce leap up of your inmost identity, a leap that takes you, if only for a second, into the freer air.'

What Gay sensed that evening was 'the freer air'. Of a spot on another Devon river he later recalled: 'I fished one moonlit night on my own here one Summer... I was in no hurry as fishing this place on my own was mostly all night. I hit a load of grilse or Summer salmon of around 7 lb. As I tied on the net after putting it in, I looked back across and all I could see was the flanks of fish in the reflection of the weir and moon, leaping out of the river, fighting the net – the sheer power of them in their prime condition fighting the net to carry on back to where they were born.'

This passage strongly suggests to me that he knew more about nets and his own fight with them than he had the language for. But he says it elsewhere eloquently enough: 'Rivers have been a big part of my life, likewise so was trouble!' His account of doing time in Dartmoor prison, for example, is all buoyancy. The defiance does not skip a beat. Closely interested in the tasks he is assigned, he plants trees, helps with the drying of hay or manufacture of pig nuts. We'll come back to this conjunction of rivers and trouble.

*

Seven centuries created a town to which net-making was a more or less a reflex, a compulsion even. To shut down the factories only altered the expression of that reflex. I don't just mean that the factories got smaller and hid away on the town's industrial estates. *Ho! Ho! Ho!* went unreviewed in the national press and, you murmur, you are not surprised, but the book raises issues which are at the moment of keen interest to economists.

Why, they are asking, does our thinking about economics continue to hang around the factory gate? Capitalism in the nineteenth century was understood as that system by which the owners of capital pay their workers less than the value of what they produce. Out of this 'extra' value, new investments grow. But how well does this account work in the twenty-first century, with employment set to grow ever more precarious, as extreme weather events grow ever more frequent?

Anna Tsing has argued, for example, in *The Mushroom at the End of the World* (2015), that 'private assets almost always grow out of unacknowledged commons'. Environmental thinkers in this vein have begun to describe capitalism as essentially parasitical. Through battening upon life processes that stretch into the remotest past, it has succeeded in cannibalising our future, too. Those factories relied, as many still do, on fuels generated by biological and geological processes acting incrementally over millions of years. Capitalists reimagined these processes as a service laid on for their own ephemeral benefit.

When seen for what it is, the scale of this conceit is barely comprehensible. A farm, say, relies on the photosynthesis of plants and respiration of animals, life-strategies evolved over millennia. Capital may co-opt these but does not determine them and never did. There is a new interest in what Tsing describes as 'pericapitalism', which is to say everything, long-standing human communities included, which capitalism may shape to its uses but does not itself generate and for which it accepts, as a matter of course, no duty of care. An 1843 report shows boys as young as six and girls not much older were working in Bridport's twine yards. In 1865, families in financial need were rarely sending their children to school for more than a year.

*

The town's pre-industrial layout is largely preserved because, even in the heyday of its Victorian factory system, much of its production was 'outwork', carried on in people's homes just as it had been before the factories. The long, narrow back gardens specially adapted for rope-making have retained their unusual form to this day. The wide pavements which are a feature of the town centre are also thought to have originated as spaces allowing residents to make nets outside their front doors.

In this way, net-making could be fitted in around the domestic schedule, carried on as the cottage industry it always had been, supplying the Victorian factories as they emerged, but never completely defined by that system. Today's smaller net-making companies still outsource production in this way. Over centuries, this was a livelihood that literally wound its way into every aspect of people's daily lives, shaping the town's layout and even its language. It was said of its inhabitants that they measured the distances around them not in yards but in fathoms.

*

Britain approaching its industrial and imperial zenith cast a glance backwards, as if for reassurance, to the age of exploration. Images like *The Boyhood of Raleigh* still testify to that moment. Indeed, if Google and its '18,800,000 results in 0.46 seconds' (currently) is anything to go by, 'we', or someone, anyway, is glancing backwards still. England was a country whose destiny lay now, crucially, elsewhere, or, rather, in the global economic system which it helped to create.

Level with that horizon, is the sailor's arm issuing an order? Is this a salute, even? Is place to be abolished with immediate effect? And if the boys are keen to obey this order, why? Or is it the rest of the world only that is to obey? Or the viewer? The Genoese is directing our gaze, in any case, to that somewhere out of sight which shall from now on be the only concern proper to a man. Our true purposes *here* shall henceforth be worked out only by reference to somewhere completely out of sight.

One reason the Victorian public was so ready for this has no more to do with sixteenth-century England than with Google. Earlier in the nineteenth century, South America overthrew Spanish and Portuguese rule only to fall at once under the control of British commercial interests. Brazil at this time, for example, has been described as an unofficial member of the British Empire and something like this was true of everywhere else in the newly 'liberated' continent.

Paraguay was the exception that proves this rule. When it sought to direct its own course of industrial development, retaining a measure of autonomy, Britain organised a 'triple alliance' of its neighbours to invade the country (at their own expense). Paraguay was quickly reabsorbed into the world system then centred on London. In 1870 it took out its first loan in the City, for a million pounds. Three million pounds were eventually spent in paying it back.

In very brief, that is how matters stood between Britain and Latin America as Millais made preparatory sketches on a Devon beach. Might I, in view of this, suggest a new title for the painting known currently as *The Boyhood of Raleigh*? What about *Career Advice for Young Walter* or *Have You Considered Banking*?

Do you feel ready, now, to authoritatively scorn Millais's image and everything it stands or ever stood for? It's noticeable, though, in the way we argue about this, how we still follow the Genoese sailor's arm. I've just done it myself. We join Millais in placing what matters outside the frame of this painting. We might call what mattered to him imperialist or kitsch but we join him in locating it on the other side of the world, or in what the sailor is pointing *to*, not what he is pointing *from*.

We aren't wrong to. That gesturing from sixteenth-century Devon beaches set in motion a wrenching planetary transformation. But what if, reading it this way, we miss a disavowed meaning here? What if the image contains also a message addressed *to* everything it apparently points *away from*? The home audience was, after all, its original one.

What if the subconscious theme of this painting is how Britain's centrality to the global system came at the cost of a profound moral dislocation? What if an inward hollowing out had to be enacted *here* as the precondition for everything that was then to be extracted *there*? Riches flowed from over the horizon, back along that sailor's arm, but brought with them a heedlessness arguably with us still, a callousness, towards our fellow-humans and immediate surroundings, both.

*

The first Bridport stood in the ninth century on a low hill between two rivers. It was one link in a chain of defended settlements built to protect against Viking attack. The hill is still there in the slope of its central streets and means little enough to those who use them today. The two rivers are also still there, but only when they flood seriously, as happens every few decades, is everyone reminded which parts of town stand higher than which others and why that matters. Its inhabitants catch sight, then, of some very elementary questions about what makes a settlement more or less viable. It is by water that such questions are returning to haunt coastal communities everywhere.

I'd been here fifteen years before flooding cut the town centre off one Friday night. In the road closures and wailing of fire engines, in the blue sparkling of police vehicles, you saw that question clearly enough. Here was water breaking and entering everywhere, blocking streets, silting up sitting rooms, shutting down markets, squatting basements.

'Rivers have been a big part of my life, and so was trouble!' Gay missed the point of his own insight into rivers and trouble, but his instinct about their juncture was right. Millais made of water an anonymous means to the end of elsewhere and thereby drastically falsified it. This is what is really disturbing about *Ho! Ho! Ho!* Gay's gleefully related exploits display our collective will to ecocide without the artificial sweeteners of industrial PR or 'heritage' with its handsome old frames. That is why he is essential reading.

The gangs were *essentially* neither a matter for the police, though they were that, nor were they the enviable anti-heroes of their own account. From this memoir they emerge, rather, as intelligence and energy thwarted and distorted, abandoned to their own devices, offered no language but that of TV, adapting the skills that history had equipped them with even as respectable capital ceased to concern itself with their fate. Will there ever be, I wonder, a room at the town museum devoted to this tricky topic?

Should there ever be, it might seek to answer the following: how far were these gangs rogue elements? Might they not be seen, rather, as the Johnny-come-latelies of a long tradition? The fabric of Bridport's town centre is witness to three or four centuries of care and continuity. That fabric is what visitors admire. But it may serve to conceal, as well. The prosperity which built this came from the town's position in a global network. A salt house by the harbour, built for the cod trade, stands there still. Directly or otherwise, much of its wealth came from those vast, now-vanished shoals of cod off the Newfoundland coast.

The collapse of that fishery figures hardly at all in the way the town sees itself. Any more than *Ho! Ho! Ho!* ever made it into the museum gift shop. But why not? Is it any wonder that some of the disposables left behind here when capital moved on adapted their skills the way they did? That they treated their regional river system as a cash machine? Hadn't everything they were from treated the world's oceans as exactly that? You didn't, it turned out, need to send nets to North America to help wipe out wild salmon populations. What Bridport for so long assisted with and prospered from remotely could, for a while, be done just as well right here.

The English rivers to which a few wild salmon still return, or try to, are choked with eutrophic growth from nitrates. Their banks are largely bare of trees and their beds are muddied with topsoil run-off from fields growing maize for pig-feed. Climate change driven by the profit-seeking of fossil fuel companies has left the sub-Arctic waters, in which salmon spend most of their adult lives, further off than ever. They may be protected by law but the Bridport Boys, as Hughes clearly saw, were not the only ones implicated in the breakdown of the natural systems on which they rely.

I am not, I repeat, offering what the gangs did for anyone's admiration. Remembered a certain joined-up way, though, they serve to dispel the countrified delusions which beset places like this. Rivers *are* trouble. Bridport's have it in them, still, to remind the town now and again of their power to disrupt. *Ho! Ho! Ho!*, read the right way, might similarly restore to us a clearer view: of the staggering conceit and organised criminality which have for so long characterised our treatment of the natural world.

Poems

RADOSŁAW JURCZAK

Translated from the Polish by Roderick Mengham

Elon Musk dies on Mars

for Ana Adamowicz

There's no pain, there's the light of sympathetic LEDs.
And hours of gazing through an armoured window
which is like watching Netflix in separate rooms,

one room is green, the other red, with no door from red
to green. It's beautiful, the way so many things are missing.
There's no pain. There's the light of sympathetic LEDs,

and there's a murmur. The transmission wheedles. It's Earth. Your Earth,
except there's no Earth: there's a view of Earth
like watching Netflix in separate rooms,

with the same pair of eyes (while all eyes on Earth
are looking at you. And what they see is: peace,
with no pain.) There's the light of sympathetic LEDs

a gesture. An airlock release. A dutiful drip.
Molecules pass through the cell membrane as if through an armoured window
(like millions of Netflix streams in separate rooms)

and now the flowered cool muslin and the ribboned snoods are bootless
along with the mars twitter transmission and the rocket that silver tube
there is no pain anywhere there's the light of sympathetic leds
like watching netflix in separate rooms.

Elon Musk honours the colonists

For Janek Rojewski

Whoever's going to trade in water or silicon ore
as butch and archaic as natural gas or gold
all huddled together on this tiny red dot as if around a camp fire

caught by a lens as if by a probe and beamed down to earth
like samples of Martian rock that wait in neat rows.
Whoever's going to trade in water and silicon ore

and is granted extended and flexible credit
like a pair of wings or a sail, stronger and bigger than earth,
all close together on this small red dot as if around a camp fire

rewarded with specie as uncountable as galaxies
they wait in an orderly queue, and listen to chirruping drones
all butch and archaic. As with natural gas or gold

unknown on earth for a long long time: with names like animal breeds
extinct a century ago, with faces like the conquistadors
all huddled together on this cold red dot as if round the seat of a fire.

Equipped with guns and dollars, they wait in an orderly line,
whoever's going to trade in water or silicon ore:
all butch and archaic as natural gas or gold,
all huddled together on this tiny red dot as if at the heart of a fire.

An extensive behavioural monitoring system is introduced in the colonies. The central module speaks:

*I have long spoken of the possibilities of creating a social mechanism modelled on the
mechanics of the heavens – so that, given the laws of motion of social bodies, as with
those of the celestial bodies before them, one could finally establish the same general
properties and principles of behaviour for both.*

Adolphe Quetelet

You will never know as much about yourselves,
            as nothing knows about you, you infrared domains
whose borders are not that prehensile; to know as much about yourselves

as nothing knows about you, you infrared kingdoms,
            you differentiable creatures in an invisible orbit,
you just don't want to know. How much the network knows about you

and, unless prompted, will not say, you caressed by a thousand sensors
            differentiable creatures in a calculated orbit,
you will never remember. The network remembers and dreams:

(and what it dreams about, you calculable creatures, you will never know:
you non-random creatures all cradled into a swarm.)

The price of water in the colonies exceeds $100 for the first time

can you think of water as the seventh grammatical case
resting unused, but always on the tip of the tongue?

Pornhub Elegies

[o]

Wherever you are, if you still exist, what are the links or
                highways that could reach you? Where was it I peeled off

and via how many loading bars did you leave that room,
                which servers took you away, if you did in fact leave,

out of the state of Maine like an empty glass ball
                did you feed the cameras with your disappearance

and eleven years later? How many Polish mirror servers did you look in,
                and how many other mirrors? I lost my mind over

the number of zeros and ones you held in your hands
                but how many held you? On how many monitors

do they fail to unsee you? In eleven years of streaming
                what dreams may come

when we have shrugged off this mortal coil?
                Wherever it is, if it still exists, like a long lost password

To an inactive subscription, will that recording ever be recovered,
                and on what servers, and will you even be on it?

I wanted to write a poem for you but this is not a poem for you
                it's as full of holes as a deleted cookie.

Nine hymns for sad frogs

/biz/

O Bitcoin exchange rate, Swallow, Lost memory cell
what desires sustain you, and what hand pushes you?

Swallow, Bitcoin exchange rate, semi-permeable membrane
between coin and hand, between whose faith

and whose desire will you steal? Non-existent swallow,
what eyes discern you, and what numbers will ensnare you

and stick to feathers like oil? where is the best perch
and water to quench thirst? in whose hands will you place your trust,

Bitcoin exchange rate, Swallow, Lost memory cells?

/g/

[The Parker Solar Probe completes its fourth orbit
around the Sun]

To continue is not what you imagined
Peter Gizzi

To continue is not what you imagined:
elliptical curves are not surprised by anything;
nor is the second time derivative surprised;
but the sun is always surprised. What is sent back to earth

is more and more surprised; transmit, you're losing momentum;
in the discharge sensors, there's an imaginary chill
you would be surprised by, Sun, if you could be surprised:
to continue is something quite different. Upload, you're losing momentum.

(The sun will not surprise them: streams in binary code
will swallow the one after the zero, adding to the clever neurons
formed of derivatives, surprise and silicon. Gazing at the distillate

they will transform it into a future, and make memes out of it.
To continue is not what you imagined;
The sun is always surprised. Transfer, you're losing momentum.)

/an/
[Adolphe Quetelet turns off the monitor]

, opposite in the McKinsey skyscraper the spreadsheets are still being fed, the Indian
from UberEats takes a longer way home than usual, the application knows about this
and smiles mournfully;

> *Therefore, these days we understand more clearly how the freedom of the human will*
> *just disappears the moment we dig below the surface of phenomena [...] we are amazed*
> *at the precision and immutability of these laws to which human bodies are obedient no*
> *less than celestial bodies.*

, the Vietnamese on Okopowa street closes the bar, the pans lying on the countertop
like sad, unwilling animals; he makes one mistake, and fails to close the door, the sur-
veillance system knows about this and smiles mournfully;

> *We will find out perhaps, how many will stain their hands with the blood of their fellows*
> *every year; how many will commit forgery; how many poisonings; with as much ease*
> *as we now predict the number of births and deaths every year... and if these phenome-*
> *na themselves show a similar striking regularity, its is reasonable to arraign the mate-*
> *rialism of those who do no more than enumerate and point to this regularity...*

, at the crossroads the night-time security arrangements at the Biedronka will change
to the daytime security arrangements of the ladybird

and this is just metabolism: whatever goes in, comes out looking different;

the barcodes know this, and they will be watching;

Note: Radosław Jurczak, born in 1991, is a Polish poet and philosopher based in Warsaw. He has published two books of poems: pamięć zewnętrzna *[external memory, 2016] and* Zakłady holenderskie: A Commonplace Book *[Dutch Betting: A Commonplace Book, 2020]. He is a senior editor for* Kontent, *a Polish journal of contemporary poetry and criticism based in Kraków.*

Jurczak's work has been widely lauded by critics and fellow poets alike; he is the recipient of the Jacek Bierezin Prize (2015), the Silesius Award (2017) and the Warsaw Literary Award (2021). His poems were featured by Versopolis.

Jurczak's poems make frequent use of sci-fi tropes: space exploration, surveillance devices, and futuristic technologies all make regular appearances. However, his work has little in common with speculative poetry – a genre that historically never gained much popularity in Poland. Instead, Jurczak – coming from a background in philosophy, mathematics and AI – has spoken publicly about his ambition to reconcile the languages of poetry and science within a thoroughly updated modernist framework.

Jurczak draws on a variety of classical forms and diverse literary traditions. Auden and Miłosz play an important role in many of his poems; the line 'and now the flowered cool muslin and the ribbon snoods are bootless' (from Elon Musk dies on Mars*) is a direct quote from the sixteenth-century Polish poet Jan Kochanowski.*

Five Poems

CAROLINE SYLGE

Small Group Gathering

I did not go.
I waited till late
to decide yes or no.

The rain may have played a part.
It was hard, too wet to wear
my new sheer skirt.

I'd been prepared to drive, to say:
just a cup of tea please.
But who wants to arrive
in trousers you've worn before,

to sit tired and listen
in another person's kitchen
while they share their thoughts,

and you try to work out
if you should or should not be
sharing yours?

That night, I did not go.

5 pm Walk at Snapes Point

There is no space in my life
for your friendship,
but the evening sun is out,
and this meeting removes the need
to drink wine or work.

We tread through poppy fields and pasture,
to pink thrift and common gorse,
where we pause,
and you sip water on a bench
while I choose to stand.

We can see beyond the bar, and the light
whitewashes the harbour
while we talk long and hard.
Our loop ends at the Holm oak,
where everything is quiet and we part.

Crush on Gabriel's Wharf

They made a nest of tulip petals
on the table top
then climbed inside to kiss.
The waitress served them wine
in miniature glasses
while they held hands and smiled.
It was just the two of them,
and better to be small and away
from the off-Thames wind –
they had to raise their heads
to see St Paul's. To eat, they made
their soup spoons into chairs,
though she slipped off hers
and moved to his knee,
framed by a mustard jar
and stray rocket leaves.
Then after talking a good while
and quite late, they abseiled
down the table cloth,
clutched each other
as if they would never meet again
and went their separate ways.

At Gaia House in Devon

I met my fear in the heavy sky
that hid the blue we knew was there,
and under the staggering oak tree
where I felt only this high.

In the owl's call on the first night,
on the bed that was not mine,
and taking toast to the lounge
with the pots of red geraniums.

I met my fear, and then I lost her,
walking through the vegetable gardens.
Lifting my feet up and placing them down,
circling the cemetery of nuns.

I somehow, somewhere, lost my fear,
and then I lost this.
I lost this, slowly,
then overnight, I lost that.

I lost this, then that,
then him, and all of them.
I was walking slowly
on the wet evening grass

barefoot alongside others
and I lost everything.
And drawing on the jacket of the breath,
I realised I was happy.

The First Murder on a Buddhist Retreat

The first murder was the worst,
under a Thai moon, in a steaming night.
By a cooler dawn, the others lay
in tiny heaps, and I serene.

Sweating on my bed, protected by a net,
I had been sleeping when she came in,
hurting my ears with the pitch
of her frantically beating wings.

We were to be up and breathing at 4 a.m,
there was no breeze,
even my parched tongue
had given up its plea.

I turned on my Maglite to locate her,
then – fingers covered by my sheet –
pinched out her chugging whine
and ground with my thumb her scuzzy body.

Fragile relief – until the next.
Inside my beam of light I took stock
as they danced against the sticky walls,
then lifted the muslin, prepared to kill the rest.

The first murder was the worst,
under a Thai moon, in a steaming night.
By a cooler dawn, the others lay
in tiny heaps, and I serene.

Poems

CHRISTINA BUCKTON

Great Auntie Nicey

*('No, not Nicey, it's Eunice, pronounced Eunicey, as in the
Greek')*

It's not for long – she can't get out – she's asked for you.
Straighten her cushions, talk to her.
So I'm imprisoned too.

She winces as I try to shift her pain –
not there, that's worse. I drop the cushion.
Clock hands creak. Nothing to say.

The boys are playing war outside – half naked, free.
Sit properly – not ladylike to loll about....
Boredom. Jaw aches. And hours till tea.

Well then – her breath a fog – *d'you want to play?*
She means the Chinese cabinet. I fumble
at its tiny doors. Now I can look away.

Open it – careful – you're much too rough,
there's something for you. Look inside.
A shilling in a nest of dust and fluff.

And how about a kiss? Her skin
is sapless, hand crawls out to mine,
stippled with blotches, tissue thin.

I teeter at the crater of her mouth
stopped by her wizened throat
and my own ruthless youth.

She sighs – *well what's the news?*
Clock wheezes into life and strikes.
She is the witch. She wants my juice.

Keep in Touch – a love letter to Voyager

A great leap in the dark into
the terrible emptiness
does anyone remember to send you messages like
stay well stay safe

On and on
no destination
buzzing round and round like a wasp in a jar
stuck there

All the stuff
we've been doing since you set off
the lovers the babies the plague while you
trog on in the dark

Burrowing in blackness
snuffling through stardust
do you wonder if we just let it ring when you called
got on with our lives

Your data
doesn't say much
like a teenager's postcard from France not wishing
we were there

Or did you forget us
long ago carelessly
breaking free from our planet leaving a note that
we hoped would say more

Maybe you'll still be collecting data
like an obedient retriever
long after the asteroid cracks us like eggshell or maybe
you threw the instruments overboard

as you stepped straight
through the firmament
exited the heliosphere carrying unopened
our love letter to the cosmos

Copper Beech

Nothing destroys the harmony of a garden more than the
  dark blotch of a copper beech
(gardening handbook *c.* 1950)

The night's gone but the dream stays, a picture
masked by tissue paper.
Here it is, the copper beech my mother planted in 1951
wearing her distinguished dark-leaved silk
disdainful
distinct
don't you forget we are the salt of the earth
Her graceful branches do not stoop down to reach me.

I would rather have been raised by wolves
hanging on to a dug dragged through brambles
than be left exposed here
unmothered
untethered
under the beech tree's pointed leaf buds
sharp as pencils
among encrusted fungi bleeding at her feet.

She is imagination's metallic colour
drawing attention to itself
refusing to fit in
we move in the best circles

I want her to say my name with tenderness
hold my hand and just be still under the sky.

But she is turned inward. She cannot do that.

At the dream's end she is not the tree.
She is a child, smaller than me.
She and I are searching for mothering.

Grandmother Gaia,
lift us both up into your branches.
We are your visiting birds
perched high together, cradling each other
with our own uncertain wings,
our hearts in time together.

The heart is an edible fruit.
Cut myself a slice
under poured light like liquid
like love

Pantry Moth

I stay
in the shadows, soft
interloper
secret as a sunflower seed
wings a fringed shawl
quietly sumptuous, folded
discreetly. I like to fit in.

I am
mouthless. I masquerade as
muesli for
my mission: multiply.
I am pulse, I am
egg machine with a soft centre
and look – motherhood!

My waxy maggots are all
mouth, they
snuggle and gobble in
the sugar bag, overrun
the oat flakes, then
outgrow themselves, burst
out of their tight whiteness
spin and swing into
cradling cocoons.

Done.
I am breathless, bloodless, a whisper
of chiffon
thumbsmudged
to a smear of dust on the shelf.

Three Poems

SOPHIE HANNAH

First and Twice

The last time I was happy, I was watching Francis Hunt
(from the website Market Sniper). He was saying, 'Get in front
of the coming wealth-destroying crash.' In words both clear and blunt,
he said, 'Stash some bars of gold beneath your bed.'

Why? Well, interest rates, stag-flation and the link between the two,
and the price of debt, the NASDAQ, what a bull is going to do
if some bears jump out of windows, and a Bitcoin surge that grew
then contracted. Then my son walked in and said

that he'd cheated on his girlfriend (on a beach in Magaluf)
though she'd cheated on him first, and twice, but then she'd told the truf,
whereas he'd just cheated once, but hadn't told her, and their youf
and the ever-present drunkness of them both,

and their lay-waste teenage hormones and their strong belief in shoulds
led to swift devaluation of all assets and all goods
and a ruthless razing to the ground of loves and livelihoods.
(Since I couldn't work, I saw no fiscal growth.)

Anyway, the point – apart from: hi, Black Friday! – is that now
I want happiness again, and, what's more, know exactly how
to achieve it: by pretending that the tragic cheating row
never happened. Take me back, please, Francis Hunt.

Tell me more about how hoodwinked libertarians secured
too much tolerance for crypto, which in turn then brought on board
all the risk-shy Stockholm Syndrome types, and everyone ignored
that the booms were just a mirage and a stunt,

and that every fiat system – sooner, later – falls apart
like my son's trust in his girlfriend, hers for him, each mind, each heart,
and I'll tell you, Francis Hunt, how much I wish that we could start
pricing in that human beings are always flawed,

and we do not have to shun them if they slip up now and then.
(When we do, we hit rock bottom like, apparently, the yen.)
So forgive your loved ones' ill-judged drunken trespasses. Amen.
(And then stay at home and never go abroad.)

Wilfred Owen Rewrites *Dulce et Decorum Est*

*Secretary of State for Education Nadhim Zahawi
denounced a decision by the OCR examination
board to replace two works by Philip Larkin and
Wilfred Owen from next year with a more diverse
range of authors, to be studied as part of its GCSE
English literature course.*

Rejected, shunned, like beggars in their sacks
(stinking, with smokers' coughs), we cursed those fools
who run exam boards, who have turned their backs
not just on us war poets, but on all schools
and every pupil who will now not learn
that war is shit (News flash: it still totes is).
Some pipsqueak said 'It's someone else's turn'.
All blame for the resulting hell is his.

Wait, what? Hey, boys. Hey Larkin – have they told you?
You might not care, but me? I'm glad I'm dead.
Young people: watch out for the lie they've sold you.
The powerful, then and now, they take your head
and stuff it full of falsehoods. Soon you're drowning
in fashionable contrivances, not free
to save yourself. Like Stevie said: that's drowning.
Take heed, Ted Hughes, Lord Byron, Robert Browning –

you will be next. If you could read the minds
of those rank vandals who would dignify,
with the word 'progress', drawing down the blinds
on cultural riches, stamping syllabi
into the dirt; dead poets, if you knew
who they were lining up as substitutes
for (soz to boast) the greats like me and you,
then – as I do – you'd crave a gun that shoots
dead even ghosts. Don't dare say something vague
About letting each new age tell its story.
Have you seen this one? It's all Molly-Mae Hague
And Tommy Fury.

Philip Larkin Rewrites Mr Bleaney

'This was Mr Larkin's page. He stayed
high on the list of English Lit set texts
for many years.' A limp-spined book, dismayed
by years of pawing by dirty fingers, next

is handed to you: an anthology
of the crushed hopes and quiet resignation
of English poets: all veiled apology
for wanting anything at all. Our nation,

its oh-so-humble people, are not great
at bigging ourselves up, taking up space.
'They won't print more of those. At any rate,
not with those Larkin poems, though they were ace.

Well, people thought they were, but only those
who stay up half the night brooding on death.'
'I'll read him,' you blurt out, half-comatose
with misplaced guilt and boredom. Soon your breath

is held while, on the same old shabby bed
in which you write the poems you pray have worth,
you read old shabby words. People have said
Larkin was sexist. Lay him, then, in earth.

Forget him. Whether he anticipated
this slight, who knows? He foresaw most sad things –
maybe not this one, though. It might have skated
well past his range of grim imaginings,

and whether one day a young poet, like you
this morning, will be told that you were dumped
by an exam board thinking it could do
better without you – though your sore heart thumped

with a fierce truth, though your best lines could touch
huge yearnings in small lives – we cannot say,
and shouldn't really bother all that much,
let's face it, since we'll all be dead one day.

Poems

JENNY KING

Shadow

My father was studying Russian. Intrigued,
I joined in, learnt a few words.
They lodge in me still.

Suppose me now lost in some Russian forest,
searching about for anyone to direct me.
Boat, I could say, and *worker, dog* and *children.*
Union of Soviet Socialist Republics
and *Not by bread alone.* But nothing useful.
Then as they stared, add *Peace* and then *Goodbye.*

What would they make of this? A madwoman
loose in the forest!
Nor would it help to know that *shadow* in Russian
can be both masculine and feminine.
As maybe shadows are.

But when I passed you, neighbour, on the stairs
and chatted a moment as we usually do,
I found I couldn't bring your name to mind.
It's true I didn't need to, but as we parted
your shadow on the wall was mocking me.

What grew in my father's garden

In the many beds he nurtured sweet peas, sunflowers
and day lilies.
My mother came out with her secateurs
to help with the roses.

In the greenhouse he sowed orange wallflowers
and forget-me-not.
My mother sat on the wooden stool
and they chatted as he worked.

In front of the house he set crimson chrysanthemums
and autumn crocus.
My mother admired them through the window
from her chair.

At the back he put evening primrose, Michaelmas daisies
and winter pansies.
Then he came in and made coffee
they drank together.

Later, weeds dotted the beds
where he worked alone.
At the end of the garden were foxgloves. The wall made a shelter.

Petersham Meadows

The bus climbs
past the Dysart Arms
just as I remember
up between the trees towards Richmond.

From the hill I look down
into my own childhood. Guernsey cows stood
among the tall grass. Behind them
like a sea-wall

slabby concrete
neatened off where the water meadows
spread out, with their ice cream hut
open on Sundays.

Once, a lone American soldier
perched on the wall gave us chewing gum,
my brother and me,
knowing it would be something new.

Looking down, I am the god of the landscape.
I see into the depths, command
how the air between is made of old shadows
flocking together into that known place.

And all the while the Thames
flows on beside the land
it would rise to cover when it chose,
as years have overflowed that distant time.

Numbered

As the wall of the house
is bricks shoulder to shoulder,

its neighbouring lawn
green blades gathered together,

the wood down the lane
a fellowship of trees,

so this hour between *now* and *shortly*
bunches the clustered minutes, to keep them

like seeds in a packet.
Except we have numbered them

one to sixty and after that
starting again from zero, the uncountable

O! O! on the digital clock, the engine
we have set

on a plain of measureless living
to show us when we are,

while God watches from eternity
our world of counted sparrows and numbered hairs.

Luciano Erba's Centenary

PETER ROBINSON

'I would like to enter history', writes Luciano Erba (1922–2010) in his later poem of that name, 'as a unit of measurement', and from this seemingly self-aggrandizing opening he improvises an informal, *arte povera* lyric with a distinctly self-ironizing close:

I would like to enter history
as a unit of measurement
Watt Volt Faraday
or else give the name to a scale
like Mercalli Fahrenheit Réaumur
mine should be the tedium scale
point one November rain
point two the evening haunts
point three, four... take your pick
and so on, up to nine, myself.

Among Italian writers' centenaries celebrated in 1922, including those of Bartolo Cattafi (1922–79), Beppe Fenoglio (1922–63), Luigi Meneghello (1922–2007) and Pier Paolo Pasolini (1922–75), all born in the year of Mussolini's March on Rome which took place between 27-31 October, was that of Luciano Erba, who entered history by being born some six weeks earlier on 18 September. (For an illuminating guide to the year of *Ulysses*, *Jacob's Room* and *The Waste Land*, nothing beats Kevin Jackson's *Constellation of Genius: 1922, Modernism and All That Jazz*, whose author, alas, died a year short of his subject's big anniversary). Around the turn of the millennium, I was fortunate enough to visit Erba on various occasions while working on *The Greener Meadow*, a selected poems published by Princeton in 2007.

The poet recently featured on the cover of *Poesia* no. 17 (January–February 2023). The issue includes an essay by Samuele Fioravanti, who edited a 2022 scholarly edition of *L'ippopotamo* (The Hippopotamus), alongside a selection of poems from the new collected *Tutte le poesie*, edited by Stefano Prandi with a preface by Maurizio Cucchi in Mondadori's Baobab series, also issued for the centenary. It makes available Erba's lyrics from the earliest, dated 1937, to those written in the year of his death, describing the arc of this 'singular, wise and acute witness', as Cucchi puts it, 'genial through the simple, incomparable rigour of his language'. 2022 saw conferences, including one at Milan's Catholic University, from which Erba graduated in 1947 and would retire as Professor of French – when his collection of literature in that language was donated to its library.

With his wife, Mimia, the poet lived in a large double flat reached by two elevators in Via Giasone del Maino, with a wide plant-bedecked habitable balcony, innumerable books, the family's much-loved cat, and his box of Meccano, brought out one day at the mention of a poem which concludes by evoking this fondly preserved toy:

you'll say birthday or nativity
it was my essay on the soldier king
the parents didn't agree
'you know very well the teacher'
'but where have I put my grey hat'
'before God for that matter'
meanwhile humble minutely Po-valley I
'I'll be late to the office'
would wait with pen in hand
and ponder on my Meccano set

'San Martino' from *The Hippopotamus*, published by Einaudi in 1989, is now the subject of a long scholarly note by Fioravanti in his annotated edition, *L'ippopotamo: edizione commentata*, published by Roberto Cicala's Interlinea. Drawing on the poet's secondary bibliography, Fioravanti reports Prandi's distinguishing between a 'poetics of the object' in Erba and Eugenio Montale's use of them. Where Montale, in the last of his 'Motets', for instance, alights on a paperweight made from a coin stuck in a piece of lava and concludes that 'life which seemed / vast is briefer than your handkerchief', Erba employs a 'programmatic absence of any symbolic intention and thus the renunciation of possible compensations of a transcendental nature'. Fioravanti concludes: the 'Meccano and Erba's other objects would therefore be "placed through imaginative activity on the same level, aligned as sumptuous fragments that markedly point to opacity, unknowability, rather than Montalian epiphany"'. This ten-line childhood memory, with citations of domestic friction, illustrating Erba's 'humility of regard', exemplifies what Cicala calls an 'impossible idyll... a lost idyll' informing the poet's entire oeuvre, and one characterised by such ironic self-portraiture as that in 'I Would Like to Enter History'.

If Pope's famous zeugma specifies stains on 'her honour, or her new brocade' not least because his father was a cloth merchant, the hats in Erba's work likely spring from his dad's employment in that industry – hats like other daily objects helping the poet to resist the abstractly polysyllabic discourse of Italian literary sublimity, occasioning too his political scepticism and religious doubt. Closing the trunk where he has discovered a present bought for a daughter while visiting a Sioux reservation in North Dakota, Erba finds a close for his poem by quoting the original English label:

Not even worn once
now it seems a chestnut purée

almost a mont-blanc, but flopped down.
And to say that the Indian girl had smiled
stroked the horse
and that the sun among the trees...
But goodbye Rocky Mountain
'hand knitted original article!'

The description of the hat, the situation of its purchase, affection for the child whom it suited, and its being found, not quite good as new in a damp country villa, all point towards emotion evoked without being stated, to how, as Wittgenstein had it, a poem's diction, even though 'composed in the language of information... is not used in the language game of giving information', underlining Erba's ability to find poetry in such out-of-the-way places too.

'Reclosing a Trunk' moves from informal evocations of incidents and objects, collaged together from widely distanced locations (a villa in northern Italy and a glade in the Rockies). This prompts memories and emotions, though ones cut off by the closing trunk, preferring not to remember with those suspension points, and an exclamatory farewell that evokes feeling about fatherhood's miscarried gestures. Erba's objects are frequently located in domestic interiors, as if the final frontier were not interplanetary vastness, but the micro-regions between things in nondescript everyday surroundings – explorations of territories opened up by Gaston Bachelard's *The Poetics of Space* (1958).

Being born in 1922 meant that Erba celebrated his twenty-first birthday just as the Italian Social Republic came into being, when Mussolini, rescued from captivity at Gran Sasso by German paratroopers, was established as the puppet ruler of what remained of Italy under Axis control. Though he preferred not to make anything of it, Erba had helped Jews escape from Milan to Como and over the border into Switzerland. When he himself was reported to the authorities, Erba, like many others, set off for the Swiss border and was interned in a work camp, a departure recalled in a section of 'Railway Suite' entitled '1943' in *L'ipotesi circense* (*The Circus Hypothesis*, 1995):

I was reading in the eyes of farmhands
my destiny my sure condemnation
in the mountains I would go
hiking boots and overcoat
I was wanting to flee
Italy and Salò

The collection includes 'Chasing Vittorio S on the Zenna Road', a tribute to the poet Sereni, his one-time high school teacher. There, of the 'shivering beech trees' and 'trembling leaves / I say it's a message, somebody receives', an answering rhyme imitated from the Italian which suggests a spiritual reciprocity between the fact of animated objects and their possible perceivers. Such responsiveness points beyond opacity and unknowability, if not quite to epiphany. The so-called poetry of objects has become a matter of reading the signs.

His internment in Switzerland prompted a number of significant early poems, including the much anthologised

'La Grande Jeanne', further exemplifying Erba's use of objects to catch with a feelingful irony the thwarted or impossible aspirations of ordinary people from his generation:

It made no difference to la Grande Jeanne
whether they were English or French
so long as they had hands
the way she liked them
she lived by the port, her brother
was working with me
in 1943.
When she met me at Lausanne
where I would stop in summer clothes
she told me I could save her
and that her world was there, in my hands
and my teeth which had eaten hare in
    high mountains.

At heart
la Grande Jeanne would have liked
to become a respectable lady
she had a hat already
broad, blue, and with three turns of tulle.

This portrait of one compelled to a life of prostitution with aspirations to better herself employs its details – hands, languages, where she lives, summer clothes, food eaten crossing the mountains, and above all that fancy hat – as significant not because they point to a meaning beyond themselves, but because in themselves they represent qualities for the people attached to them. Pasolini pointed out in 'Implications of a Linea Lombarda' (a poetic grouping that got its name from an anthology including Erba published in 1952) that it 'does not represent the prophecy or destiny of an epoch Montale-fashion, it lives in a deliberately minor zone made of delicate illuminations, tender surprises, ironies à la Prévert, jolts of the heart'. Erba's earlier poetry was collected in a 1960 Mondadori collection pointedly entitled *Il male minore* – that's to say, the lesser evil.

In an essay on Pierre Reverdy, Erba finds 'a reality lightning-struck in the instant that precedes life's metaphysical equation', a spirituality in images created by bringing remote things together. He similarly associates far-fetched items under humble headings – as when in 'Any Old Cosmos' comparing as 'without design' the 'necktie for my birthday' with 'the eastern block's *Trabant*' motor car. Erba frequently effects such collocations with homophonic puns, as in 'Sad Plays on Words', where 'tassi' (yew trees) around a hospice occasion a 'lettera tassata' (one with excess postage to pay) inviting the collection of a dead relative's personal effects. This carries into the final line's 'splendido pennello di tasso' (a splendid badger-hair brush, or, when read out loud, Torquato Tasso's splendid shaving equipment). For his annotated edition, Fioravanti consulted manuscript remains lodged at the University of Pavia, discovering the poem's original title to be 'Tassonomia' (Taxonomy). Needless to say, such internal poetic logics aren't easy to translate.

Concentrating not so much on objects themselves,

then, as on what's between them, Erba evokes indeterminate spaces and non-places, moving simultaneously inwards and outwards to suggest the possibility of a beyond, as in 'The Metaphysical Tramdriver':

Sometimes the dream returns where it happens
I'm manoeuvring a tram without rails
through fields of potatoes and green figs
the wheels don't sink in the crops
I avoid bird-scarers and huts
go to meet September, towards October
the passengers are my own dead.
At waking there comes back the ancient doubt
if this life weren't a chance event
and our own just a poor monologue
of homemade questions and answers.
I believe, don't believe, when believing I'd like
to take to the beyond with me a bit of the here
even the scar that marks my leg
and keeps me company.
Sure, and so? another voice *in excelsis*
appears to say.
Another?

Fioravanti finds here a continuing dialogue with Sereni's poem 'The Alibi and the Benefit', set on a Milanese tram one foggy evening where he remembers Erba's poem 'Tabula rasa': 'in fact *it's any evening crossed by half-empty trams* / *you see me advance as you know in districts without memory* / never seen a district quite so rich in memories / as these claimed to be "without" in the young Erba's lines'. If 'The Metaphysical Tramdriver' is in such a dialogue, again poetry's lyric solitude reaches towards others and an afterlife, affirming and doubting, just as in 'Tabula rasa' the lines simultaneously deny and enrich a place's memories.

Erba's work employs objects and the links between them to signify themselves, give shape and form to lives, represent other things and values, and as in one of his very last poems, 'Hunting for Images', to evoke, again by not attempting to name, an all but inexpressible distinction:

Mystery, we see you from the corner of our eye
we brush by you, perhaps on truth's outskirts
    already
putting a hand to the forehead
there emerge many images
we imprison in a net of words
if instead you hold chin between thumb and
    forefinger
the net remains empty, two plus two's four
a bit like the difference
between a woman passing by amidst flowers
and the same who, still in springtime,
passes, wherever, though not through flowers.

Thus, to the end, Erba was finding in poetry ways to catch at the mysteries of existence, mysteries never far from the truth of things, which can be glimpsed by attending to minute differences in contexts where we experience the colours, substances and spatial forms of our days. In a world more characterised by mendacious certainties and hardened false convictions, Luciano Erba's poetry has much to teach about how to regard the world in which we are obliged to live with a tender pathos and wry humility.

Poems

RICHARD PRICE

Jogo do Bicho

Numbers from the Brazilian gambling game and their Animals

1. Avestruz (Ostrich)

Head in the dust. Braves all weathers.
Optimistic dinosaur. Diva feathers.

2. Águia (Eagle)

To see is to kill.
God's first drone, if you will.

3. Burro (Donkey)

I've a fence to scratch against
and a mouth full of thistle.
I could sing! Or hum.

Or whistle!

4. Borboleta (Butterfly)

Fancy a flutter?

5. Cachorro (Dog)

I used to be a wolf way back when.
I lived with the pack up on the hill.
I came down to laze around
and promised not to kill.

6. Cabra (Goat)

My life is drastic.
It's hard earning a crust.
I chew fly-tipped plastic
and unrequited lust.

7. Carneiro (Ram)

I'm used for the ewes –
something to do
with who or what I am.
(but I've been a woolly thinker
since I was a lamb.)

8. Camelo (Camel)

If you carried freight from neck to rump
you'd spit pints and take the flaming hump.

9. Cobra (Snake)

Armless.   Not harmless.

10. Coelho (Rabbit)

No fox for me,
as luck would have it.
I live a charmed life –
magician's rabbit.

11. Cavalho (Horse)

The flames on the cave wall
were horses.

12. Elefante (Elephant)

Presence.

Absence.

13. Galo (Rooster)

I am the man.
I am the police.

                    (*He is the soup*).

14. Gato (Cat)

Transaction, friendship, love.
All... or none... of the above?

15. Jacaré (Caiman)

Wasn't me
but I'd better lie low.

16. Leão (Lion)

A mullet haircut and I'm king.
All the ladies do... is everything

17. Macaco (Monkey)

I'm on the last remaining tree.
I used to walk the forest, branch to branch.

Their gods are cars, tv stars, a vast cattle ranch.
They make a human out of me.

18. Porco (Pig)

Just one purpose in life death.

19. Pavão (Peacock)

All eye the dance and the dance eyes all.

20. Peru (Turkey)

I vote this Christmas
we stuff ourselves.

21. Touro (Bull)

Civilization – dancing on the back of a bull.

22. Tigre (Tiger)

We will escape the stripes of this cage.

23. Urso (Bear)

Now I've stopped dancing for you
you miss your own cruelty.

24. Veado (Deer)

beneath the forest trees
sunlight and shadow

pause

25. Vaca (Cow)

I want to be free
of my sole identity:
motherhood.

Richard Price writes: *Jogo do Bicho*, 'the animal game', is a form of lottery found across Brazil. It is illegal federally and in almost all individual states and it is vastly popular. Each number is associated with a particular animal. This is a convention that goes back to how it all started, in 1892, as a means of funding Rio de Janeiro's Zoo (and no doubt funding its 'enterprising' owner Baron João Batista Viana Drummond). At first the lottery took place at the Zoo itself, with each ticket representing one of twenty-five animals presumably kept there. Animals such as cows and rabbits, who feature in the list, were of course originally exotic to South America; the Zoo also had entertainments for children so perhaps these help explain the presence of more prosaic creatures in the game.

    I have been interested in Brazil since a school project in primary school when I learned of the city of Manaus, so far inside the Amazonian interior. Since 1999 I have worked on books with the artist Ronald King who grew up in Brazil. In 2009 I was lucky to visit and tour the country on the back of launching my Selected Poems in Portuguese, translated beautifully by Virna Teixeira. Some time after my return, Ron began talking about the clandestine game as a potential new project, but we both became side-tracked and the project didn't take. The game seldom left my thoughts, however. This may be because it occupies in my mind a kind of perpetually unfinished 'bestiary' – that genre which I guess began as a descriptive list of animals found in secular illuminated manuscripts before becoming a specifically poetic form (I think, for example, of Apollinaire's *Le Bestiaire ou Cortège d'Orphée* with woodcuts by Raoul Dufy, and of the Aardman animation *Creature Comforts*). More than that, 'occupying the mind' is something that the animals themselves seem to do, and I was not immune to it. This is exploited by the printers of the many

Brazilian guides designed to interpret dreams and other psychic events that may feature animals – not to reach a deeper psychological understanding of the dreamer (Freud is so slow, so non-functional, my darlings!), but, rather, to help the lucky reader choose the right numbers for the next lottery draw. My bestiary here is meant to, well, 'capture', something of the animal and of the human as they play, willingly or not, their life gamble.

For further context there is an eye-opening book on the subject I can heartily recommend: Amy Chazkel's *Laws of Chance: Brazil's Clandestine Lottery and the Making of Urban Public* (Duke University Press, 2011). Chazkel contrasts the chancy speculations of the ruling classes of which Drummond was a member, where the risks they take are seldom existentially personal but can affect large parts of society at the burst of a bubble, with the ubiquitous, small-scale betting world of the animal game. While *Jogo do bicho* was originally designed to fund a private zoo, soon notorious for its poor treatment of the animals in its care (you just know that the money was never going to go their way), it became detached from its first intent as middlemen moved in and copied and popularised it country-wide. *Jogo do bicho* was briefly legal but soon criminalised, threatening as it did various kinds of vested competition, though the law preferred to state moral reasons for banning it. Nevertheless, the beast, as it were, had escaped from the zoo and it has never been recaptured.

My boast ኢትዮያዊ ነኝ!!

BEDILU WAKJIRA

Translated from the Amharic by Heywot Tadesse and Chris Beckett

I am a churchgoer in Lalibela, pilgrim to the tomb of Sheikh Hussein in Balé,
a man showered with blessings by the Abba Goda as I water my camels,
one who receives my *Rizk* in Mecca, and the nephew of Burjo in Hamer.
I am always rich because God loves me. I earn exactly what I deserve.
Nobody denies me what is mine. I do not take from anyone unless they take from me.
I celebrate New Year with Chambalala of Sidama and Giyta of the Wolayita,
as well as in Saint John's in Addis Ababa, marking Advent down the ages.
In my totality, I am invincible. In my parts, incorruptible.

Who am I?

I live in the mist and frost of Sannete, the ice cap of Mount Dashen.
I walk the dust storms of Dollo Mena and the lava soup of Dallol.
I raise my cow in Yirgalem and mate her in Wollega, truss and milk her
and taste the first cup of her milk in Axum, and with this northern milk
I fill an Arsi chocho to the brim and churn it in Gambella, before I rush
across to Harar to anoint a famous beauty with the butter.

Who am I?

Footloose as a grasshopper, I spring up in the air when you think I'm dead,
circle back the long way when you take me for gone.
I am tormenting as sunstroke, unrelenting as night terrors.
I have no walls, no fetters. Too big to fit in a village or a town, I am the size
of a country and no tribe can define me except to say I am human.

But who am I?

I farm my land, till my soil, guard borders, defeat enemies.
My plough is never unyoked, my waist always holds a round of cartridges
and a Lee-Metford always hangs on my back. I return affection
with affection from the abundance of the harvest and if you are insolent
I will answer you with gun powder.

Who can I be?

I am stubborn as a mule, effective as a termite.
I never shrug off a grudge.
I carry myself like a monument to the Battle of Adwa, upright
as a freedom flag in Rome, and everything I do, I do barefoot, as I was born.
The ways of Christ are my ways, too tight to be measured or dissected
    with cunning or dissembling.
I am an emblem of faith, an icon of solidarity, invincible, incorruptible,
a man who is presented with frankincense in Jawle and a ton of myrrh from Ginir,
gifted with khat in Aboday and bags of coffee beans from Aba Jufar's Jimma,
served the three little cups called
                    Abol, Tona, Baraka
            for *Pleasure, Contemplation, Blessing,*
a man who is sung the Wadda in Soddo, who chews khat all night long in Gode
    and breaks his high with a glass of camel's milk
while he ties the flag of his country round his neck as an amulet.

So who am I?

Footloose as a grasshopper, I spring up in the air when you think I'm dead,
circle back the long way when you take me for gone.
I am tormenting as sunstroke, unrelenting as night terrors.
I have no walls, no fetters. Too big to fit in a village or a town, I am the size
of a country and no tribe can define me except to say: *he is human.*

Who am I?

I am an Ethiopian!
        I boast in many voices!

Tongues of Fire: Eric McElroy in Conversation

GREVEL LINDOP

Composer and pianist Eric McElroy's forthcoming CD from Somm Recordings, *Tongues of Fire*, features his settings of poems by Gregory Leadbetter, W.S. Merwin, Alice Oswald, Grevel Lindop and Robert Graves, sung by tenor James Gilchrist.

McElroy has written for solo piano, voice, choir, orchestra and various chamber ensembles; his work has been performed internationally and he is currently working on a commission for the English Symphony Orchestra. He has recently been researching at Merton College, Oxford, where this conversation took place on 31 January 2023.

GL: Eric, I know very little about your background. Could tell me how you got into music, how you started playing – indeed, where it all came from?

EMcE: I started playing piano when I was three. My mother's a piano teacher, so that's why I began so early, and I've been playing piano ever since: I can't remember a time in my life when the piano wasn't there. I did an undergraduate degree in piano performance in Washington State, then went to Vienna, where I did my Master's degree, and afterwards to the Royal Birmingham Conservatoire – because I wanted to do a degree that focused on British piano music, the repertoire of early to mid-twentieth century; then I came to Oxford to do a research degree on that repertoire. That's sort of the elevator summary. But yes, I'm a pianist-composer or a composer-pianist. For me they're one and the same.

GL: And how did you begin to compose? Have you always composed from childhood?

EMcE: It would have been very early, between four and five, something like that. There are tape recordings somewhere in my parents' house of things that I'd written at that age, and I've been composing ever since. I'm a completely self-taught composer: I've never taken a composition lesson in my life.

GL: Truly?

EMcE: Once you master how to play an instrument, you really just need a library card and a CD player and the world is your oyster: you can figure it out on your own. I think that I wouldn't write the sort of music that I do, I don't think it would quite be *me* if I'd done a composition degree. I think I'm just the sort of person who had to figure it out on my own.

GL: When and how did you decide that you wanted to set poetry?

EMcE: It would have been around the age of sort of thirteen, fourteen when I started experimenting with setting words to music. It became a central part of my work as a composer from... well, from about 2012 onwards. I love music and I love poetry, and this is a marriage of the two, so this is the best way of putting those things together.

GL: Your doctoral research has been on John Ireland and his interest in Arthur Machen – a writer who specialised in the weird. You seem to have an interest in the uncanny or the weird in some of your own work. I'm thinking of the Gregory Leadbetter sequence on your forthcoming CD – *The Fetch* – and in a way the Graves poems too; and I think you cited Graves's work including *The White Goddess* as some kind of catalyst for some of what you've done.

EMcE: 'Catalyst' is the right word, I think. I was at that particularly impressionable young age when I'd never encountered someone who was such a radical thinker, or such a free-thinking person – Graves expanded my idea of what was possible. I fell in love with his poetry: it spoke to me and it opened the door to other poets and I love his work. I feel personally addressed when I read his stuff. It's that sort of connection you feel with a great writer.

GL: How old were you when you first discovered Graves?

EMcE: I discovered him first as a translator in *The Twelve Caesars*. I would have been in eighth grade, which would put me at twelve. The poetry followed within a year or two after that.

GL: Is *The White Goddess* an important book for you as well, or less so than the poems or novels?

EMcE: It's one of those strange great books that just change your life in some way you can't quite articulate. There are some books like that that you read – they're so distinct, so powerful, they just *breathe* off the page – so I read it right through.

GL: Can you say what it is about a poem that attracts

you to the idea of setting it? Are you looking for an effect that it has on *you*, or something in the structure?

EMcM: I think about this a lot and I make no progress with answering it. But there's one thing I can say about *before* that, though... The subject matter of a song cycle, say, can precede my reading or discovery of the poetry. With *The Fetch,* for example, I knew that I wanted to write about something to do with ghosts even before I'd met Greg; and then I went out searching, trying to find poetry to match this nameless feeling that I had. I wanted to write about something that I couldn't even put into words. And then you'll read a book and say 'That's it.'

GL: So clearly you find poems that *reflect* something that's already there within. There's some kind of Platonic process whereby there's a recognition, an anamnesis, rather than just discovering something out there and thinking 'Ooh, I d like to set that!' Maybe that happens sometimes as well.

EMcE: Right. I mean, sometimes I'll read books of poetry and I'll have the thought, 'Oh, I could set that one to music', and I'll bookmark it and maybe someday go back to it. But first you have to have that drive, that need to do it.

GL: Reading critical discussion of song settings suggests that there's often an assumption on critics' part that the composer is bringing out something already inherent in the poem. So that it's as if the poem is primary, but the composer's job is to see what hasn't been fully expressed, and to pull it out.

EMcE: You're right: that's an opinion that comes up quite a lot.

GL: In reviews they'll say that the composer 'brings out' or 'makes explicit'...

EMcE: 'Highlights...' Which I don't like for multiple reasons, but the two on the top are that it seems the poem is somehow insufficient without the music, and then, two, it assumes that the reader is not keen enough to sort these things out for themselves. With some poetry those things could be true, but I'm looking for something that can obviously stand on its own. It doesn't *need* me to set it to music, but *I* need to set it to music When you listen to a song setting, you're not hearing the 'true' version of that poem, or the amplified heart of that poem, you're hearing my reading of it; so you're also learning something about how *I* read poetry.

GL: What are the goals and constraints when you're setting a poem? Can you articulate a sense of what you're trying to do, and what the difficulties are in doing it?

EMcE: Well, there's probably a more interesting answer. But more surface level questions that you have to consider are simple things like phrase length. And, you know, the limit of how long a singer can sing.

GL: Of course, yes.

EMcE: And sometimes – like for your poem 'Mirror and Candle', for example – the phrases in the poem are quite long, and so it becomes a challenge for the composer: 'How do I show the length of that thought, while still giving the singer the space to not feel completely out of breath?'

A lot of composers veer towards poems that have shorter phrases. Because it matches the voice. It's something that one wouldn't think about as a poet because it doesn't matter.

GL: Well, clearly I didn't.

EMcE: But actually that is reflected in the way I set it. That song has this wonderfully *long* sense of line, that I think I successfully reflect in musical terms. So, simple things like that. But what I'm interested in is reflecting the feeling that's beneath it. How do I translate that into musical terms? What I feel when I read that particular word or that phrase?

GL: In the sequencing of your CD there seems to be a progression from these very eerie meditations on liminal aspects of nature and consciousness from Gregory Leadbetter, continuing into the quite mystical late poems of Merwin, followed by the maybe more tactile poetry of Alice Oswald. Then the love poems, and finally the Graves war poems – early poems where the war is often reflected in nursery rhyme, ballad forms, childlike conceits which turn very dark.

EMcE: Greg Leadbetter's 'Misterioso' I think makes a natural opening, in the relationship between music and language which it discusses. My Merwin cycle might be the most disturbing; I was struck by Merwin's obsession with the absence of self. There is a sense of loss and resignation in these texts that just hurts. A poem like 'The Morning' is terrifying, ominous: it has the horror of feeling somehow inevitable – which is heightened by the incantatory form of Merwin's poetry.

GL: And there is the one poem by Alice Oswald, 'A Short Story of Falling'.

EMcE: I'll never understand how Oswald can have been the Oxford Professor of Poetry since 2018, and yet there has not been a single collaboration between her and Oxford's Faculty of Music. Talk about a missed opportunity! Even more shocking is this: my 'A Short Story of Falling' is the first art-song setting ever done of Alice Oswald's poetry. The piano and vocal parts are full of water imagery. I wanted to convey the sense of power and the ecstatic that emerges from our contemplation of water. I have flagged other poems by Oswald as potential song settings, but these are waiting for someone to come along and commission them.

GL: Turning to my own poems, I was astonished that you'd managed to create a sequence out of poems that were written almost half a century apart. You'd picked a poem up from more than forty years back, put it along-side two that were written much more recently – and they seemed to work.

EMcE: Yes: but to me, say, the landscape of a poem like 'Mirror and Candle' is the same landscape – although dealt with in a different way – as your poem 'Bed' from *Luna Park*. I mean, one is clearly from an older perspective, the experience that is covered in that poem, whereas 'Mirror and Candle' could be written at any age. But from a reader's perspective it doesn't feel like something that was clearly written decades ago. Maybe it concerns how one's texts speak to each other across the years. For me the sequence of those three is like, the 'Watching' opens the erotic scene that we're on, with two individuals; 'Mirror and Candle' is the space where these things happen, it's the bedroom space and it's the light and feeling; and 'Myth' is the act itself. To me they make a natural set of three.

GL: Yes that's what's so interesting: you've created a coherent sequence from disparate poems.

EMcE: Greg said something similar about *The Fetch*: he said it was like a little book, out of his own: he'd found it interesting how I'd made a sequence out of it, that at the same time reflected the whole of his collection in miniature. And that was really gratifying to hear from him and also to hear that sort of comment from you: because that's certainly how I feel about the cycle. A poem like 'A Dozen Red Roses' I think will be anthologised as one of the great love poems of our time.

GL: I actually found it quite difficult to summon the courage to publish the first and third of those poems, and they may well be the poems that I would have been most frightened of ever having performed in public. And you have *unerringly* hit upon them! To me it's actually quite frightening. An intimacy coming out to such an extent.

EMcE: I had similar thoughts about it. But one of the things that I wanted to accomplish when I wrote the *Tongues of Fire* cycle was: so many poets and poems and so many songs and operas write *around* these subjects and it's all metaphor. I wanted something that didn't shy away from what we're actually talking about, but did so in a way that wasn't lurid but that was joyful in a way. But I guess maybe it's one of those things, sacrifices, you make as an artist that you are putting parts of yourself out there.

GL: You are your own material.

EMcE: The only person who could have written songs like that or poems like that must be someone who has lived deeply and not only had experiences like this but who was able to understand them and to translate them into these sorts of mediums. And to me that's a gift.

GL: That's interesting. Sometimes when I've been helping people develop their own writing I've had to say, 'All good poetry or much good poetry when first encountered has something slightly embarrassing about it'. I've said this because people writing poetry will often shy away from a key aspect of the subject, because they feel it's too personal or somehow too intense. And yet often that is the essence of the poem they're trying to write.

EMcE: It's the same with composers.

GL: And what it's about is that you're becoming your own material: your lived experience – which is really *you* – becomes your art. That makes you vulnerable.

EMcE: This is a distinction that I try to draw in the notes for the CD: this distinction between art as autobiography and art as *me*. I see this with a lot of other young composers, where I can't see the human being in what they're doing. Or it seems like it's all intellect or cleverness or something, and I'd rather have these other things. Many of the things that I've written that I like most are those where I got rid of any filter and asked myself, 'Why not?' And when I've asked that question, most of the time I can't find a good answer. So I go for it.

GL: I found that kind of intensity in some of your Graves settings.

EMcE: I mean, 'Strong Beer' is such a rousing finish. It ends with a bang. I find that poem, and the way that I've set it, sort of terrifying… It brings out the animal in one, the frightened animal in oneself.

GL: Yet it begins as – apparently – the hearty Georgian, praising beer and country inns.

EMcE: Those last two lines: 'Teach me to live that I may fear / The grave as little as my beer' – to me this wasn't a joke, this was a desperate plea. That sense of manic desperation in face of the terror of death is what I wanted to bring out.

GL: And 'Here they lie': only four lines, with this disturbing last line – 'They were true men, they had pride.' I keep rereading that line. It's got great impact, *strange* impact: what's meant by that?

EMcE: The last word in particular: I placed that last word – 'They were true men, they had' – and then the 'pride' is separated. When I read that poem it made me think of a statue in a desert, it had that coldness. It reads like a monument.

GL: It brings this weird stasis at the end, doesn't it? And the implicit question I suppose is also 'How will I, *can* I, match this – where am I in relation to that?' you know.

EMcE: It's surprising to me, with Graves's enormous output and his influence on twentieth-century writing, how relatively little he's been set to music. There are not as many songs as you might think; certainly not as many songs of great stature. There's a cycle, *Wild Cyclamen*, by Hugh Wood which is quite good – ten of Graves's late 'muse' poems – recorded by, also, James Gilchrist actually. But other than that there's not much Graves setting of stature. I don't know why. The publisher has certainly been very accommodating.

GL: Can I just ask you which composers of songs you admire yourself?

EMcE: I'm wary of these questions, because even if only subconsciously it compels us to approach the music of one composer through the music of another. I listen to music from all over the place and not just classical music, and I've learned just as much from reading poetry, memorising poems or listening to other people reciting poems, as I have from song setting. So many young composers in particular – when I say young, I'm thirty, but my generation and younger – they don't read. They don't read poetry, they're not engaged with the other arts in the way that you wish they were. I don't know why this is. I think this is a cultural shift.

GL: Maybe there's a tendency in all areas for people to get boxed in with one particular pathway. Maybe it's something to do with the way things are communicated now. There isn't a broad or an interconnecting interest.

EMcE: I wish that these two worlds went together more often. I think poets doing creative writing courses should be learning about the history of song setting. It would teach them so much about the history of their own art form. And *vice versa*: composers should be forced to take an English course!

GL: And do you have any future plans? Or simply the intention to continue with composing and performance?

EMcE: I'm going to do this till I drop.

PNR at 50: supplement

COMPILED BY JOHN McAULIFFE AND ANDREW LATIMER

PNR

ROBYN MARSACK

Like Brighton rock, the name MICHAEL SCHMIDT is embedded in *PNR* whenever you bite it. The name is the quality mark, from the editorial in issue 2 of *Poetry Nation*, in 1974 (his name was absent from no. 1), to issue 271 of *PNR* in 2023. Issue 6 in 1976 announces a new format, new frequency and that 'we' will be joined by new editors, Donald Davie and C.H. Sisson: the editorials will be 'unsigned'. So in 1977 there is a whole new gang: the General Editor, the new editors plus Brian Cox, James Atlas as American Editor and Val Warner as Assistant Editor. Soon the editors decide to sign their editorials, taking it in turn to lay down gauntlets. In 1979 the trio of Schmidt, always the General, Davie and Sisson are unsupported for a while; co-ordinating editors come and go throughout the magazine's history. The editorial that caught my eye in the Archive is Sisson's from 5:5: 'One of my worries about this magazine is that it is not doing enough for the suppression of *what is called poetry*' (my italics). The cover acquires an illustration in 1980. By 6:6 (but the numbering doesn't settle reliably until a few years later), Michael is apologising for its late appearance, citing the 'hundreds of letters' received in the wake of the special issue, *Crisis for Cranmer and King James*, guest-edited by David Martin. The cover changes back to text only.

On they go, the indomitable three, producing another special issue in 1983. This one features photographs of 'The Battle of Little Sparta', another kind of authorized version from a Scottish source, Ian Hamilton Finlay. They're joined by 'Contributing Editors': Dick Davis, John Pilling and Nicolas Tredell. Having joined Carcanet in 1982, in autumn 1983 I contribute my first piece, on the Cambridge Poetry Festival. It is so magisterial in tone that I feel it must have been edited by Michael to remove all the hesitations and qualifications I would have advanced as a novice. In 1984 the whole issue is given over to *Some Contemporary Poets of Britain and Ireland*: 'an attempt to describe the contemporary work that most engages us – that most engages me, I should say', Michael writes in a brief editorial. 'My fellow editors would doubtless have made different and probably shorter work of it.' Those editors depart after the following issue, remarking that they have 'helped or hindered the General Editor with critical comment, mostly after the event' and are relieved to be giving up writing editorials 'sustaining the illusion' that there was a 'collective editorial mind'. Michael responds that *PN Review* has 'not lived up to their hopes, though it is perhaps better than they expected', but reiterates his 'considerable personal debt' to the older poets.

Very occasionally after that, Michael would hand over the reins to a guest editor: to Clive Wilmer for a Cambridge Poetry Festival issue at the end of 1985 (that year I was a co-ordinating editor, along with Michael Freeman – but that didn't mean we had any substantial say in the contents of the magazine, certainly not in the choice of poems included); in 1986 to Nicolas Tredell for an issue on the 'new [critical] orthodoxy'. Mike rose to be a general editor alongside Michael for three years, and in 1986 Stuart Hood, Gabriel Josipovici, Ruth Morse, Mark Thompson and I were listed as Contributing Editors – this reflected Carcanet's strong fiction list. I can't quite believe that Michael Abbott (then the Sales Manager) and I were allowed to edit no. 56, but I see that 'Poetry Live' was in fact a publishers' promotional volume and I've no doubt that Michael didn't want to be associated with choices of poets he hadn't made himself.

We all disappeared from the masthead in 1990, when Michael apologised for misprints due to a new way of generating text, and advised that a new design would be coming in – which it did with no. 75; one of those austere – let's say it, downright boring – cover periods was beginning. A redesign in 1993 somewhat improved the text-only cover, and Neil Powell began his long stint as a Co-ordinating Editor. Images made their cover appearance in 1996.

Some elements of editorial responsibility were devolved to the fine Carcanet editors of the new century: Judith Willson took on the role of reviews editor for a couple of years from 2004; Eleanor Crawforth managed the News & Notes 2006-13; Helen Tookey became Co-ordinating Editor from 2011 to 2015, when Luke Allan came in as Deputy Editor and revolutionised the design and the covers (the latter had been tweaked with colour blocks in 2005). By this time the editorial address had been the Corn Exchange, the University of Manchester, Manchester Metropolitan University, depending on the institution which gave Michael his living wage; the University of Glasgow (the difficult green place), St John's College Cambridge (bower of bliss), and back to the seat of Carcanet.

The title 'General Editor' was dropped in 2019, and in 2020 John McAuliffe's name appeared below Michael's, both as Editors, with Andrew Latimer as Editorial Manager (he'd arrived as Production Manager in 2017), and new Contributing Editors Vahni Capildeo, Sasha Dugdale and Will Harris. For the essential job of proofreading Maren Meinhardt was given credit in 2022.

In no. 269, Michael writes that 'with each issue, PNR editorials become more exacting. After so many efforts I am increasingly in peril of stepping into the same elegiac river twice…'. Say 260 editorials over these fifty years, thousands of poems sifted and chosen, the scope of each issue set, the commissions, the correspondence – and then a Press to run, and teaching to engage with, fully. Whether you agree or disagree with those editorials and choices, often deliberately provocative, across fifty years Michael has been constant in his service to what *he* calls poetry: a unique and magnificent achievement.

Having a Drink

MILES CHAMPION

What surprises the most is the exceptional good grace and humour with which Michael continues to do everything he does – a remarkable feat, given the particular world he has chosen, and made, for himself. Equally rare is his respect for those whose tastes and enthusiasms are contiguous to that world. To single out one generous act from many: early in 1994 he asked me to review *Eternal Sections* by Tom Raworth, knowing I would welcome the opportunity to express my admiration for the book. I sent the review to Tom – not without a good deal of nervousness – and our friendship began. Happily, my friendship with Michael continues, some thirty years later. Besos y un gran abrazo, Michael! Come visit us in Brooklyn! Forgive this bauble, if you can!

Having a Drink with Kingsley Amis

after Wendy Cope

PN Review is turning fifty
And some kind of party seems vital.
I know this isn't much of a poem
But I dedicate it to Michael.

Kind Emperor

ANTHONY (VAHNI) CAPILDEO

I've never fallen in love with a photograph. The static image just doesn't do it for me. How do faces blossom? Eyes widen and brighten, or grow pensive and downcast? What do the hands say?

It's hard to write about Michael Schmidt. To fix a form onto one of the liveliest beings I've ever met. Can the words *constant* and *mercurial* fit into one sentence? A constantly listening heart, and incessantly switched-on brainpower.

Something in me danced, on learning that my new University of Glasgow boss was Mexican. The sun on the other side of the world, the awesome awareness of pre-Columbian cultures, formed his interior landscape. His wicked playfulness and elegant erudition took on a more approachable air. I felt unspoken comfort that another hemisphere homed us both. For him, too, body language and frames of reference were endlessly in translation.

So. Here are three scenes. Movement. Not album leaves. Not vignettes.

One. I'm a new lecturer at the University of Glasgow, and Michael Schmidt lets me use the attic office he's leaving. Mineralic, oystershell, demi-sec light pours in through the window. There is an amazing collection of books, and with boyish generosity, Professor Schmidt turns to me, wanting to give me as many as I need or want. He wants to hand on a tradition, the chance of conversations with the living and the dead, and it's still an ache that precarity made me refuse these precious companions, unsure where or how long I'd be able to house them; yet I feel as if the ideal library anyone might have has been bequeathed invisibly to me.

Two. The night is Fenland blue, and Michael and I are seated next to each other at a big table of writers in Sala Thong, a restaurant near the Faculty of English in Cambridge. It is time to talk poetry, but – upset by unexpected long-distance cruelty from a London friend – I direct a subdued wailing at Michael (who doesn't even know the guy): 'I thought he was nice and silent like a giraffe'. We browse giraffe pics on my phone, till Michael tempts me to contemplate okapis instead: 'They have much nicer bottoms'. The velvety stripes cheer us up, and I reconnect with my 'writing mind' in all its creaturely silliness.

Three. I am in Belfast, and the airline meant to take me to England has failed; failed entirely, as a business; no planes. I happily board the ferry to Liverpool, instead of a fuel-burning devil-bird – but what to do on arrival, where to stay, since my main work payment won't come through for another few months? Michael opens his Manchester home to me, with angelic promptness; I can arrive at any hour. Michael's kindness knows no bounds... good, for I'm due to read in Manchester the following night, then take the red-eye bus to Gatwick and another plane to Trinidad... This is my publisher: my brother of hemispheres, as kind as we should be to strangers.

All Hail Michael Schmidt!

ALICE QUINN

Steadfast, wise, energetic,
loyal, and dear, a fount of taste,
a beacon in the field, our hero!

CONGRATULATIONS!

With gratitude and endless admiration,

The publisher is the poet

SuAndi

I look at you
And think
With despair
Borne out of affection
Why
I have missed so much

Mischief sits on your upper lip
Wisdom in your chin
And elegance is the essence of your mind

I imagine
Not with a lover's regret
Time past is gone

Forever
Is too long for a lifetime
And if only belongs to
Wistfulness

Yet if only
In the eighties
When maturity opened its arms
You had been there too
To embrace me in welcome
So, the nineties would have been
As naughty as middle age should be

Why I call Schmobe Schmobe

KATE GAVRON

Michael is British but he is also Mexican. For a long time he represented the north of England in the BBC's Round Britain Quiz. A listener once complained to the BBC, asking why the north had to be represented by a Mexican; were there no sufficiently knowledgeable Britons to be found? When Michael received his OBE in 2006 for services to poetry it was after he became a Fellow of the Royal Society of Literature. Perhaps in anticipation of the current emphasis on diversity, his response was to say that he was changing his name to Schmobe Frsl, 'a suitable name', as he put it, for the publisher of such a culturally diverse list. I have called him Schmobe ever since. My admiration and affection for him grow every year, as fast as his beard and my hair grow white.

Letters

JON GLOVER

Oh the attic! Oh my attic!! And, since I am no longer physically capable of getting up there to sort books, papers or anything, Oh my kind helpers who found the following letters, and more, from Michael Schmidt to Jon Silkin, and to me. The first to Jon Silkin might now seem strange and unusual – they later fell out for sad, difficult and lasting reasons – but here the tone is friendly and supportive. The letter to Jon Silkin refers to books that I reviewed in *Stand*, Vol. 14, No. 3, 1973. That issue also contained work by Norman MacCaig, Ken Smith, Marilyn Hacker, B.S. Johnson, Judith Wainwright and two pieces by Terry Eagleton. The Carcanet titles reviewed show the press's capacity to be involved with poetry and poets of an astonishing range.

The number of books I had to consider in just one review was demanding. And much, including Peter Jones's Penguin *Imagist Poetry,* I found inspiring. The books, *PNR*, *Stand* and the intimate vital links between writing and editing are with me still, fifty years later.

These letters were in normal typescript from that date. I have reproduced the layout and fonts from 1973.

Letter from Michael Schmidt to Jon Silkin

23. vi.73

Dear Jon

I just now 'by chance' (re-reading the latest Stand) saw Jon Glover's <u>excellent</u> piece on Peter's Imagist book and our two HD books. May I please have a voucher copy of the magazine for our files, since it is a special Carcanet Issue in view of all the reviews of our titles! The only copy I got was my normal subscription one.

It would be nice to know Jon Glover's address so I could write and thank him for the British Poetry Review (which was the most balanced and intelligent that book received)

and this Imagist review. Peter is relieved to read it – the only other review that has appeared is the savage Grigson piece in the TLS.

Hope all is well chez Stand.

Best wishes

Michael

[This letter was forwarded to me by Jon Silkin, founder-editor of *Stand*, with the hand-written note 'gave it him' i.e. Glover's address to Michael Schmidt. –JG]

Letter from Michael Schmidt to Jon Glover

27.vi.73

Dear Mr Glover

It was very good to read your review in the penultimate Stand of our critical book, British Poetry Since 1960; and equally pleasant to read your considered and I think objective notice of our HD books and my colleague Peter

Jones' Imagist anthology. After the sadly partisan savaging of that book in the TLS (the only other review it has had), and of our British Poetry book almost everywhere, we were particularly glad to read something balanced and assessive.

I'm enclosing a brochure describing a new periodical venture we are launching. I wondered if you might at some juncture be interested in writing for it? I'm also enclosing our trade catalogue and taking the liberty of putting you on our mailing list.

Again many thanks. Your reviews are always a pleasure to read.

Yours sincerely

Michael Schmidt

The new periodical venture was *Poetry Nation Review* which became *PNR*.
Jon Glover

Michael Schmidt and *PNR*

KIRSTY GUNN

Can I think of anyone else who uses the conditional form in such an elegant and instructive manner? Making of a tense not used nearly enough in these days of opinion bashing and summative demand a suggestion both of the fun of a thing and also the darn good reason for doing it? No. I can't. Only Michael, I think, commands this part of speech with the charm and efficacy its grammatical status suggests. And commands it, in particular (I myself might say), with reference to possible submissions for certain issues of *PNR*. So, then, an 'Oh yes, I should think so...' comes in ready response to some idea about whether one might do something about this poet or that. Or there is a 'I would have thought...' that arrives in the inbox or conversation by way of a gentle sugges-tion that one is slightly off-piste and might change track a tad. And there is also the compellingly suggestive: 'Might it be the case, do you think...?' At which point one braces oneself for a powerfully imagined thesis taking in a new line of enquiry that begs a rewrite of the entire article one has just filed or embeds within its modest content vast potentials for further reading and thought – all of which, naturally, might, just, yield ideas for further pieces for the magazine, and, of course, for life. Altogether, Michael's conditionals... *sing*.

Happy Birthday, dear Michael's *PNR*! Happy Birthday to you!

Small (and Large) Kindnesses

SASHA DUGDALE

A few years ago when I was editing *Modern Poetry in Translation* and despaired of ever composing anything of my own, Michael seemed to sense this and wrote to ask if I had any work for him to see. I had nothing in the potato sack, apart from a few mouldy tubers, and I didn't know how to answer, but equally didn't want to betray his faith in me.

I had written a piece a while before and I sent it to him, saying that it was too long and wouldn't suit and he wouldn't want it, but to my surprise Michael replied to say it would do nicely and proceeded to publish it in *PN Review*. This was the long monologue poem 'Joy', written in the voice of Catherine Blake, William Blake's widow. Without Michael's enthusiasm 'Joy' would almost certainly never have seen publication.

At another point Michael sent me a book to review, a strange and glorious book, but one which I was hopelessly ill-fitted to write about. Instead I wrote as a response an essay about seeing and perspective. There is no one else who would have taken that essay in place of a sensible review – but Michael did, and I subsequently heard from readers that it had found its audience.

Last year when the war began, I put an exiled Russian poet in touch with a young British translator to translate anti-war poetry. At the time it was hard to publish work by anti-war Russians, and some editors had made it clear to me that I could only submit work by Ukrainians. Michael, however, grasped the humanity of the situation, and published the translations. This publication meant a huge amount to the poet, and it launched the career of an emerging translator.

Michael also published work by a Ukrainian poet, who had put their own fine work aside to translate and advo-cate for other poets and scholars who had been affected by war, and he took time and pains to respond with care and thoughtfulness.

These few small examples show how much good an editor can do when they approach literature and art with empathy and generosity. I have been repeatedly grateful and touched by such attentions over the years. They show an increasingly rare regard for the person behind the work, and the complexities of production, especial-ly in our straining times.

Boot Camp

DAN BURT

The train to London pulled out of Manchester Piccadil-ly in early afternoon. From our backpacks Michael and I, facing each other in a second-class coach, pulled thin sheaves of A4 covered in typed text and blue marks – scribbled comments, excisions, commas, colons, semi-colons, dashes, slashes, ubiquitous question marks. I, white-haired, the elder, unsheathed a red flair pen. Michael, the one who'd made the marks, began to speak.

This was not my first rodeo. Betters had been editing my prose for fifty years, from college to uni to lawyering in the US, Britain and the Gulf. Hundreds of professors, senior lawyers, peers, subordinates and clients had cri-tiqued my drafts thousands of times. Though I'd only begun trying to write poetry determinedly a few years earlier, and till now had sent none for publication, sure-ly five decades being blue-pencilled was preparation enough for a brief session to shape several hundred words in five pieces of halting verse. It was not.

Michael smiled, picked up *Sie Kommt*, my reverie in sonnet form about a teenage love. He complimented a line – *I thought* 'She came around the corner of the years' *was wonderful* – then bent to his autopsy. Too many com-mas, he said – he'd struck six from the fourteen lines – semi, full colons and dashes; they slow the reader's eye and ear. Use them sparingly; rely on line breaks and word valence for pace and rhythm.

He axed conjunctions and prepositions because, I learned, they're the essence of prose. They dull a poem's imagery, the vehicle for its emotions and intensity; parataxis is poetry's engine room. (I looked *parataxis'* meaning up later.)

Michael told me to reproduce a sound, rather than name or describe it, that onomatopoeia was a form of *show, don't tell.* Similarly he suggested describing mea-sures and smells with metaphors readers could envision or sense: a football field long rather than 100 yards, a car's width rather than six feet wide, the time to hard boil an egg rather than 7 minutes, the acrid, cloying odour of skunk road-kill rather than stink.

Longer poems he cut ruthlessly, his reasons faultless; *less is more* came alive under his blue pencil. For awk-ward phrases he proposed revisions, new lines, or exci-sion. He fingered faults of logic, grammar, inconsistent imagery and mixed metaphors. His judgment was unerr-ing, and I accepted all or almost all his edits, or was spurred to find alternatives when I rejected his.

Michael edited my poetry often after that first session, and always left it better than before. From him I learned the worth of arrows absent from a lawyer's quiver: rhythm, rhyme, repetition, parataxis, silence, of too little rather than too much, of a simple image like *Petals on a wet, black bough*, and much more.

If I'm even half a poet, Michael made me so.

Jeu d'Esprit

(for Michael)

ANGELA LEIGHTON

A garden's a place for talking, so much we agreed,
talking of this and that, love, poems, piss –
then how to write about it,
that functional loving ingestion of (acid?) rain
returned more benign (and alkaline) to earth.

And you, beating about a bush to find a place –
the urethra's busy push that keeps us live
recycling – thinking too
how a poem that's mostly piss might also pass
for one line saved, years later, from a scrap of manuscript.

Don't throw anything away, you said. Now look
I saved your words, recycled, not to take the mick
but thanking you, heartfelt, for wisdom, wit,
for thoughts concurred, contrary – all the fun of it.

Eggs Florentine

REBECCA WATTS

The year was 2013 and I was shivering at my desk in the Rare Books Reading Room, cataloguing the papers of an eccentric Victorian polymath as per the terms of my employment, when the door swung open and a distinguished-looking, cheery-sounding gentleman strode towards me. 'I hear you're a poet', he said – Adam Crothers, who also worked in the library, having dobbed me in. 'Why don't you send me some poems?' Well. Breaks don't get much luckier than that: the editor of the UK's best poetry magazine and publishing house walking up to you, offering to read your poems, which he has time to do because the college you happen to work for is also currently employing him as its Writer/Editor-in-Residence. The timing was especially fortunate. I'd been writing poems in a semi-focused way for a couple of years, and had a set of twenty or so in a document that I'd recently put together with a view to entering some pamphlet competition or other. Feeling decidedly squeamish, but with an awareness that I had very much more to gain than to lose, I attached the document to an email.

Dear Michael... An appropriate opener, given the kindness, instruction, encouragement, inspiration and spontaneous amusement I've derived from a decade's correspondence with the beloved Professor Schmidt OBE. Following our first scheduled meeting in Patisserie Valerie, where Michael drank three Americanos while galloping through the many interests and objections he'd noted in my document, I revised the poems and sent back the eight he'd liked most, which were subsequently printed in *PN Review* 212. For me, this was officially the start. During Michael's two years in Cambridge we enjoyed numerous jolly breakfast meetings at Bill's, and the occasional college dinner, accompanied by other wonderful poets newly adopted into the *PNR*/Carcanet family: Adam Crothers, Claudine Toutoungi, Alex Wong. There was a genuine sense of community, with Michael at its heart. Since his residency came to an end, we've missed him.

Looking back at that first set of comments he gave me, I find – as well as Michael's characteristic empathy and humility – the fundamentals of editing outlined: 'What I have done, excessively, is suggest where I think there is a runover of language and the suggested changes I hope respect the intention and the prosody, and are tentative anyway. The urge is toward a riskier parataxis which leaves more constructive space for the reader, sometimes, though some will strike you (all may strike you!) as ill-judged.' Ten years on, I channel these insights as I edit my own work and the work of others. Happy birthday *PN Review*: making space for readers everywhere since 1973.

Upwind

MATTHEW WELTON

I get up from the table and turn off the radio and as the silence settles around me I figure there're radio waves still coming this way and upwind there'll be the transmitter and a radio station, where in a room full of coffee cups and heaps of typing paper there's a needle inching in on the centre of a record.

Upwind of that in a recording studio somewhere, as a cello player nudges the notes into being, there's the sense of something definite making way for something undefinable.

A striplight fizzles. The rug unravels. The fruit bowl's too full of satsumas.

And further upwind in the schoolroom by an ocean where the composers create the hollows the notes will fill, a woman in a workshirt takes a pencil from a jam jar and breathes deep as she allows a thought to form.

I rinse out the coffee pot and boil more water; my mind slips into a melodic lull.

A spider plant thrives in the kitchen window. In either direction a cyclist goes by.

A Nice Bit of Obit

CAROL RUMENS

It's not the first thing I read when I open *PN Review*. My eye slides to the left to scan the contents list, and see if I'm going to meet enough old pals to be permitted to stay in my comfy slippers and jogging-bottoms. Next, I take a quick bracing dip into the Editorial, knowing I'll come back later for the slower, closer reading it's owed. And then comes the dream-state of News & Notes, and my favourite yew-shaded walkway – the obituaries.

It's fitting that there's no specific signpost. Death is News, of the most ordinary and the most shocking kind. The *PN Review* format equalises death-news with events like award-winning, and it tends to equalise reputations. Comparison is underplayed. Insularity is questioned. The poetry-enablers as well as the poets are honoured.

Of course, I experience a stomach-turning jolt at seeing familiar names – poets I know slightly or, more likely, since I know few poets, poets whose work I know. But, in a melancholy kind of way, I enjoy seeing the architecture of a life and a life's work compressed so elegantly and finally.

I take obituaries more seriously than I take reviews, or perhaps less impatiently. The critical assessment is not so exact as to exclude a non-reader of the work. Although usually an enthusiast for the subject, the obituarist is a reticent one. There's no need for market-credible hyperbole. The obit confirms its status as a medium of trust.

The scope of the *PN Review* obit is a major asset. It's like an international conference, where you're awed to shake hands with major writers you have never heard of. I'd heard of Friederike Mayröcker but only looked

into her work after being seduced by Jenna Schmidt's description, in her obituary (*PNR* 260), of 'ravelments filled with memories, feelings, artistic influences, reminiscences both real and imagined, an accordion-like overlapping of time and place...'. I was ready to be intrigued and stimulated by the poems and, as it turned out, the glimpse of Mayröcker's ruthlessly intense personality. She has become one of those poets I read to remember what writing poetry really tastes like.

A little added pleasure lay in the fact that Mayröcker was old – ninety-six – when she died. At my age, the older someone else dies the better. If they're almost twenty years older than I am, I'm instantly convinced I shall live another twenty years (at least). If they're younger than me, I feel compassion, and even a trace of survivors' guilt.

This was true in the case of another poet I met in *PNR* 260. It was the South African Chris 'Zithulele' Mann (1948–2021). Remembering him, Chris Miller wrote 'I have met few men I admire more'. After I'd read about Mann's life and looked up some poems on his beautifully organised website, I felt an extraordinary, profound wish that he were still alive and writing. He's one of the poets I read to remember that poetry doesn't mean being kind only to words.

A poet's light doesn't go out the day they die but death may hasten the burn-down. It's an old-fashioned metaphor, but poetry isn't on the National Grid, and Keepers of the Flame are essential. Good obituarists tend the flame. They keep it burning and they hand it on.

For Michael

ALBERTO MANGUEL

I can't remember when we met for the first time but I remember our conversations about childhoods in remote places, Canadian poetry, Dante and Milton, Gilgamesh (I hadn't read his masterly book on the epic then but have now), Greek and Roman epigraphs (nor had I read then his equally masterly book on the ancient Greek poets) and of course, about *PN Review* and the Carcanet poets, most of whom were unknown to me. Perhaps there were not more than a few conversations, but in my always creative memory they seem legion because every time I read yet another issue of *PN Review* I feel I'm having one more conversation with Michael, and learn something more about the infinite library he carries in his mind. Especially these days when the *New York Times* cautiously warns its readers how long it will take them to read an article (do you have two minutes, four minutes, six minutes to waste on this?); when a prestigious reviewer announces that Olga Tokarczuk's *The Books of Jacob* is too long for a savvy reader of today; when the British Library Crime Classics carry a warning *ad usum*

delphini letting its audience know that the authors of the thirties and forties use language that some might find inappropriate; when the Dr Seuss books are bowdlerized and courses on Ovid's *Metamorphoses* at several colleges tell the students that they can skip the class if they feel that scenes of rape might traumatize them, I rejoice in knowing Michael and following his work that celebrates with intelligence, quiet erudition and wit the freedom of the truly creative human mind.

In his introduction to his book on the early Greek poets, Michael notes that we inherit a 'fragmented legacy of ideas and figures, stories and histories that can be as real to us as our own more immediate past'. All of Michael's work acts as a showcase for such legacy, translated into our own tongue and reflecting our own faces. 'Even its strangest elements', he writes, 'rise out of the darkness almost with the force of memory.' 'Almost': the adverb is luminous proof of Michael's revelatory eye.

Thank you, Michael. And Happy Birthday, *PN Review*!

Contributors' Notes

BILL MANHIRE

I always read Contributors' Notes in magazines, which may be why I noticed that a writer had appeared twice in the Contributors' Notes on the last page of *PNR* 268. The entries were differently worded, the first longer and more detailed than the second.

This made me recall how recent this section of *PN Review* is, and how the magazine has frowned on such things over so many decades. There were Contributors' Notes in the early *Poetry Nation* years – 'GEOFFREY HILL'S first collection, *For the Unfallen* (1959), has been reissued by André Deutsch, who publish *King Log* (1968) and *Mercian Hymns* (1971)' – but biographical notes of any kind were entirely gone by the time the first *PN Review* appeared in 1977.

Back they came just a few years ago, but often as a random selection. *PNR* 268 gives us seventeen names from about twice the number of writers listed on the Contents page. Neither Contributors' Notes nor its occasional variant, Some Contributors, make it across to the online version of *PN Review*, presumably because they are already missing from the Contents page of the printed magazine. Certainly they always feel like an afterthought, included if space permits.

I find this odd because regular features like 'News &

Notes' at the front of the magazine build a strong sense of company and commonality, especially in the brief acknowledgements of deceased poets. Those pocket obits ought to be depressing but they always leave me oddly encouraged. Other people have devoted their lives to this unlikely activity!

Organising contributors' notes must be hugely time-consuming for a busy editor. But one thing we all know about Michael is that he relishes being busy. It's more likely that he considers such notes a form of marketing-cum-gossip ('puffery' is a pejorative he sometimes uses). I can also imagine him simply pointing out that the notes take up space actual poems could occupy.

I'm aware that if Michael were faced with a request for a biographical note he might hardly know where to start. Separate entries would be required for poet, anthologist, translator, critic, scholar, editor, publisher and – the looser callings for which many of his authors are especially grateful – literary activist, bridge-builder, horizon-scanner. You would need many, many pages for every category. In fact you would want the ongoing reach of what he has so eloquently brought into being with *PN Review*: the full run of it, the fifty-year astonishment, the whole shebang.

Like Wine through Water

SINÉAD MORRISSEY

I don't read a lot of poetry. I can't. A hopeless multi-tasker, I can usually only concentrate on one poem, one book, one poet at a time. I get easily overloaded.

In 1999, I returned to live in Belfast after nine years away, having missed out by a matter of months on the chance to vote for the Good Friday Agreement. I was in my middle-twenties. I had published one collection with Carcanet, moved to Japan, got married, fallen ill, stopped writing altogether, moved to New Zealand, been ambushed by home sickness in the wake of a peace process I had never really credited before, and now I was back. A new beginning, then, for me, and for the country I'd been born in, simultaneously. If I was ever to start writing again, it would be here.

What did I know? Very little. But a great deal of that little, I gleaned from the pages of *PN Review*. Poems in *PN Review* – solitary poems on their own, by writers I didn't know – showed me what was possible as I started the painful, arduous, stop-start process of beginning to write again.

I rented a flat in Merville Garden Village with a snot-green bathroom and no central heating. I worked as a receptionist for temping agencies. I earned £100 a week. *PN Review,* Volume 25, no. 6, July-August 1999, fell through the letterbox. And I read this:

They said, 'Why do you want to go to that place? There is nothing to see.'

And this:

We met two young salesmen from Usak who sang for us on the summit
Of the fortress rock, which was black but patterned with brilliant lichens.

And this:

We went south through fields of roses, their perfume smothering the valleys,
Rising up in gusts through peaks like broken knives.

The wide format of *PN Review* ensured John Ash's 'The Anatolikon' was delivered whole, in the solid unbroken block of itself, its rolling lines intact. I hadn't read anything like it before. Precisely observed and crammed – beautifully but also hopelessly – with what had already been lost. A poem singing its own redundancy, as perhaps all the best poems do.

And it struck me how respectful the layout was, how much care had been taken to house it appropriately, which was an act of generosity, to the poem and to the poet, obviously, but also to its reader, me.

John Ash's 'The Anatolikon' is just one example.

I've read poems in *PN Review* which, to quote Cathy in *Wuthering Heights* speaking of her dreams, *have gone through and through me, like wine through water, and altered the colour of my mind.*

Like *PN Review,* at fifty, too (how did that happen?), I've read single poems within its pages that have lasted half my lifetime.

Special friend

GILLIAN CLARKE

Special friend to scribblers the likes of me,

who scrawl in the backwoods obsessively,
as words went winging through cyberspace,
you gave to our writing a stage, a space.
So much would be lost were it not for you,
Carcanet Press and the *PN Review*.

In Person

ANDREW WYNN OWEN

It was in late 2016, after an event to celebrate the life and work of Elizabeth Jennings, that Michael took me aside to give gentle thoughts on a batch of poems.

The sheaf was neatly annotated, with buoyant ticks and neutral lines. He had many things to say about them that I immediately recognized as true, and hadn't thought of myself. The best criticism includes remarks that stick with you, as a writer, because it cuts to the heart of something about your practice, and perhaps even something about your life. There was plenty of that, and it was all delivered with perfect tact and concision.

When we were done, he stood up, smiling: 'Now, have you met Priscilla Tolkien?' And there she was, full of benign encouragement and stories about her father, the author of my favourite books from childhood. It was a lovely sequence of experience. It wouldn't have happened if it weren't for Michael.

It hammered home something I should have known anyway, but is a thing easy to forget: the remarkable literary figures (and who is more 'remarkable' or 'literary' than Michael?) can, in the best cases, be as wonderful in person as they are by reputation.

Puckishness and Joviality

EVAN JONES

I spent the month of September 2005 settling in Manchester – beginning a PhD in Art History I was barely prepared for in a city I was barely prepared for. There was paperwork and the filling out of bank forms, mostly, and queues. Weeks of this. Daily walks to the university to figure out something – and a queue for the privilege. This was in order, that wasn't. By October – though it was Christmas before anything was sorted – I felt I had to do something else. I went online and saw that a poet named John McAuliffe was teaching at the university. John was also, if I remember right, a recent migrant to the city. We met for coffee and talked poetry in a small fry-up place on Oxford Road that may still be there, just north of the Whitworth Art Gallery. Was it my suggestion or John's? I didn't know many places. It was good talk, though, and it has led onto almost two decades of more talk. John asked if I was going to hear Les Murray read that afternoon. This event was organised by Carcanet at the Central Library. I hadn't known anything about it, unconnected, but moved things around – queueing – so I could go.

This brought me to Michael Schmidt. He met us – he seemed to be shaking hands with everyone – at the room door at the library. He was puckish, jovial, complaining to strangers like me that Murray read too quickly. I had read *Lives of the Poets,* purchased remaindered in Toronto, and seen the occasional Fyfield Books edition in bookstores (though never Carcanet books, now I think of it). I knew who Michael was, sort of. I didn't know about *PN Review*. That came later, once I'd met him on my own and he'd asked if I'd review for the magazine.

When I think about *PN Review*, I think of that afternoon and my initial impression of Michael. One of the reasons I left Canada was because I felt it had no room for a poet trapped between cultures as I was and not at all comfortable in just one. What I found when I read *PN Review* and explored its history is a place for the range and variety of poetry. There is room in its pages for different cultures, different ideas, for puckishness and joviality, but also praise and complaint. It reflects the energy that Michael Schmidt has always contained within him and presented to others.

Michael Schmidt

RACHEL MANN

The first time I had lunch with Michael I was terrified. Through my old role as Manchester Cathedral's poet-in-residence, I had, in passing, already met him. On that occasion, he had warmed to my love for the Book of Common Prayer and wanted to talk further. However, when he invited me to lunch, I rather panicked: lunch with Michael Schmidt, the great publisher, and editor of *PN Review*? In my head, his very name was raised up in titanic block capitals. I was sure I was about to undergo, over pizza and a blood-orange fizzy soda, the most horrible interrogation, part-university entrance interview, part-essay tutorial.

The Michael I met and, of course, have since come to know and love, was no grim intellectual or terrifying don. Certainly, I was both exhilarated and knackered after that first proper meeting. We'd spoken about all the things you might expect: poets and poetry old and new, modernism and formalism, the Book of Common Prayer and the King James Bible, as well as God and the state of the Church of England. However, while all of that talk mattered, I was blown away by something else, something I began to grasp about Michael's abiding character: his joy, and his intellectual curiosity; his generosity and capacity to attend to the things that matter. Over that first lunch, I started to understand that while Michael has, as an editor, a fierce passion for the stuff he loves, he is determined not to be doctrinaire or intellectually priggish. It should come as no surprise, then, that *PN Review* reflects that generosity. His is not the default, easy generosity of a liberal, but reflects a kind of hard-won grace. The range of poets, including me, that Michael has published in *PN Review* is sure proof of that. The acuity and attention which he brings to bear as an editor is a kind of love and friendship. His kindness is beyond question. I'm glad to call him a friend.

I remember Michael...

PHILIP TERRY

I remember how delighted I was when Michael accepted one of my first reviews for *PNR*, a mediocre piece as I remember it, on Muriel Spark's *Collected Stories*.

I remember one of the first times I met Michael in person, at a launch of my *Dante's Inferno* at the London Review Bookshop. He introduced me as 'one of my least original authors'.

I remember when *Dante's Inferno* received a Society of Authors' Travelling Scholarship, Michael ribbing Neil Astley about the state of his shoes at the awards ceremony.

I remember at the Carcanet at Fifty celebration at the National Centre for Writing in Norwich, several Carcanet poets describing how Michael had meticulously edited their first books, and saying that I'd never had even a comma changed in mine.

I remember spending the evening with Michael and Jazmine, and that I suggested to Michael that *PNR* ran a Supplement on Oulipo to celebrate their sixtieth anniversary, and that it came out the next year, on their sixty-first anniversary.

I remember the poet Simon Smith telling me he had met Michael to discuss his Catullus translations in Manchester, and that Michael had shown him the manuscript of my *Shakespeare's Sonnets*, saying: 'What do you make of *that*?'

I remember at the Goldsmiths' launch of my version of the *Epic of Gilgamesh – Dictator* – alongside Jenny Lewis, that Michael embarrassed me by reading the most explicit scene, in front of Blake Morrison, where Enkidu is seduced by Shamhat.

I remember Michael giving a talk on Aztec poetry at Essex, and how inspiring it was.

And I remember Michael giving another talk at Essex about the origins of Carcanet, at Oxford, which began life as a magazine, and *PN Review*, which started out as *Poetry Nation*.

I remember telling Michael about my mother's time at Queen's University Library, where her boss was Philip Larkin, and Michael entertaining the idea that I might be an illegitimate child of Larkin's.

I remember the poet Chris McCully telling me that he'd met Michael in Manchester, and that he'd described me as a genius, though he has never said that to me.

I remember Michael telling me that when he had met the Queen on receiving his OBE, he had told her that he was her only Mexican poetry editor, and that she replied: 'You don't *look* Mexican'.

I remember when Michael was an external examiner at Essex University, when I was Head of Department, and that he said I was the most unlikely person to become

Head of Department.

I remember how impressed our Graduate Secretary was that Michael had met the Queen.

And I remember Michael telling me a story about the first time he had met Robert Lowell – in Lowell's bedroom, with Lady Caroline Blackwood – which I can't repeat here.

Schmidt, upriver

GREGORY O'BRIEN

Passing the great cities of the world –
Ranana, Koriniti – poetry was

the vehicle rolling down
the Maori road –
                Atene, Hiruharama – the green

dormitory and four-part birdsong,
the cherry orchard
                as it was. This much,

mid-stream, the writing arm gathers,
          as the ferryman does,

white horses, a river's dark breath,
this much the writing.

(Whanganui River, Aotearoa/New Zealand, July 2014)

Ping-Pong & Lightning Speed

MICHAEL AUGUSTIN

Poor Sujata Bhatt was in the frustrating ping-pong state probably all young writers have to go through: sending out a book-length unsolicited manuscript of their poems to publishers – only to see it bouncing back to where it came from. At first, naturally, she tried publishing houses in the USA where she had lived for most of her young life after her family had emigrated from India. After graduating in 1986 from the far-famed Creative Writing Program in Iowa City where we had met and fallen in love two years earlier when I was a fellow in Paul Engle's International Writing Program, Sujata had come to visit me in Bremen, Germany. Now her focus was on publishers and magazines in Europe, mailing out the manuscript or selections from it to Ireland, Scotland, Wales and England. In those pre-internet days that involved far more physical activities than today's one-click email submissions. Print out the script, get an envelope, or rather two, one self-addressed with an international reply coupon attached, write a cover letter, walk over to the post office, buy stamps, put it all into the box and hope for the best. Unforgotten the pain it caused, when instead of the letter of acceptance, the manuscript showed up again, accompanied by a more or less polite pre-fab statement of rejection, if the publishers proved to be courteous enough. (But then again who wants to read it anyways. I don't know a single writer who has felt encouraged by the insult of having his or her manuscript refused....)

This serious ping-pong game had been going on for

quite a while and when Sujata had flown back to Connecticut to see her family, I decided not to break the bad news to her on the phone should once again during the time of her absence any of her poems come boomeranging back to my Bremen address. Alas, when it did happen, I just tore open the envelope, took out the handful of Sujata's unwanted poems and decided to send them to an editor whose good old German name had struck me when I was leafing through a handbook of poetry magazines and publishing houses in Britain and Ireland: Schmidt! Of course, I didn't have the foggiest idea how Mr. Schmidt, PN Review, Corn Exchange, Manchester usually dealt with unsolicited work sent to him from other parts of the English-speaking world – but surely, considering his family name, he wouldn't ignore an envelope stamped in and posted from Bremen, Germany. No sooner said than done, I wrote a nice wee cover letter telling Mr. Schmidt about my discovery of a remarkable young Indian poet and fired it all off across the Channel. My 'ping' was done, Mr. Schmidt's 'pong' came in lightning speed: 'Is there more?' he asked. Time for me to confess to Sujata by long distance call that I had dared to meddle with the privacy of her mail. But when I delivered my punch line and quoted Mr. Schmidt's question – everything was forgiven. Yes, there was more. Much more. The rest is literary history.

Honey

TARA BERGIN

The bee was asked to say just a few words to convey the generosity of the flower. Impossible, said the bee. That's like asking a poet to summarise all the goodness of Michael Schmidt in just a few drops of honey.

Tongs in Hand

RORY WATERMAN

Where to start? *PN Review* provided my first serious introduction to contemporary poetry two decades ago, when I wouldn't have believed that my relationship with the magazine, with Carcanet, and with 'the ebullient Schmidt' (not my words, but they'll do) and his colleagues would become the most important of my writing life. Here are two quickfire personal recollections, from a mental stockpile of hundreds, many of which are meaningful because they are personal, and will remain so. All the same, I hope you'll excuse the self-indulgence.

First: the time he gently encouraged me, in one of my earliest, greenest prose pieces for *PN Review*, to jab a little harder in a short, barbed essay I'd written on a Very Important Poet – a poet I greatly admired then, and still do. Not long after, at a function attended by my editor, my subject, and (in a lesser capacity) me, Michael slid up to me at the buffet and, tongs in hand, joyously whispered that the victim of my (still gentle) admonishment 'is not amused'. I have since met the poet in question several times, and on very warm terms, and this little article has never come up. He'll read this piece, I suspect, and it still won't get mentioned.

Second: the time I met Michael from a train, before a Carcanet function in Nottingham. 'I've just been reading the most wonderful typescript', he said, as we galloped down a wet road towards a pub in a cave. 'Oh, whose?'

He stopped, looked at me. 'Yours!' When his edits and suggestions for the collection came, through email, he wrote that it is 'a remarkable book'. This has nothing to do with *PN Review*, not directly, but Michael was the first person to show such confidence in my writing and potential, when I had none in myself, and without his enthusiasms, occasional cautions, sagacity, wit and faith, I might have given up before I really got started.

Michael is an exacting and gutsy editor – as all editors should be, and to an extent that few really are. His enthusiasms are staggeringly broad: *New Poetries* is the perfect title for the Carcanet anthology series he co-edits, for poetry is a thing of pluralities, and Michael is interested in just about all of them, or so it seems. He has probably had a more profound, enduring, positive effect on poet*ries* in this country than any other person this past half-century, and will continue to do so for a good while yet. *PN Review* is testament to that plurality of praxis and thought, that vision and enduring mission. I won't claim this screed to be the apotheosis of that, but I'm honoured to have the chance to put a little of what I think, what I know so many poets and readers think, on record. Here's to *PN Review* at 100, when we'll all be dead. If the planet hasn't burned, his still-growing legacy is sure to have become an enduring one.

Mr Schmidt Stops the Mongol Army

a machinemade poem on the 50th Anniversary of *PNR*

BRANDON-OLIVER-MACHINE 2023 WORKED BY JOHN GALLAS

a book dipp'd in pohutukawa
& worth a pretty penny

page 50 is a large sonnet
in 73 languages

borne by Mr Schmidt
to terrific proportions

no debe pasar he says
phoar go the horses

anyway they all get lost
in a lemon hwyl

you khan't beat a bloody good pome
& so say all of us

To Dearest Michael,

PARWANA FAYYAZ

I met Michael, in my most unpoetic time –
In a not-so-unpoetic place. The year was 2017,
I had just joined Trinity College, as a PhD student.

We met at a poetry reading.
A new stranger to Michael, I approached him.
Eavan Boland brought us together.
We thought to know each other, then.

He handed me his card. I gifted him, four poems.
Forty Names included.
He gifted me back, courage. Wrapped in shapes,
Larger than the universe in the *PN Review*.

Forty Names made history. I wrote poetry again.
He touched us *all* in the soul – with his bright eyes,
And the brightest heart – and believing in it all.

PN Review at Fifty

JEFFREY WAINWRIGHT

Whenever I think back to the earliest days of *PN Review,* or *Poetry Nation Review* as it was first styled, my mind is clouded by a kind of anxiety that now seems comical but was a real fantasy at the time. I had always thought of myself and my work as 'of the left', and though I was a dilatory activist I had no doubts as to where my loyalties lay, while I was much less sure which vanguard was likely to lead the people into the silo of peace and justice. The more zealous of my political acquaintance indulged my dubious commitment, though they would have preferred my poetry to have a more *proletkult* timbre.

Michael Schmidt was clearly of a very different stripe – far from a Marxist, he could not even be described as *marxisant.* His co-editors included C.B. Cox who had been driven rightwards by the *enragés* he had encountered at Berkeley, Donald Davie whose credentials were rumoured to have proved less than revolutionary at Essex, and C.H. Sisson who had the temerity to use the word Tory.

What could come of publishing in such a magazine? I was quite well-read in the political history of the twentieth century and so my anxieties went something like this. Sometime after the revolution some commissar in need of something to do would review the contents of now defunct magazines such as *PNR* and notice that 'poets', once thought namby-pamby but harmless, had appeared in this iniquitous counter-revolutionary journal. I would be asked to account for myself by one of my zealous old acquaintances in a dark chamber deep below Manchester's Arndale Centre, and cravenly apologise for betraying the Revolution. My fantasy would go no farther, for it was the rigorous interrogation about being part of the problem rather than part of the solution that loomed largest in my humiliation.

Nothing I have published in *PNR* has resulted in such a penalty. In the years since I have every reason to be grateful not just for my appearances in the magazine but for its regular arrival on my doormat containing such a wide variety of poetry and comment. Nor is its value confined to current issues. I find interesting pieces in the furthest reaches of my shelves whether by accident or deliberate search, for instance Donald Davie's 'Note' on Non-Conformists and C.H. Sisson's essay 'A Four Letter Word' [Tory], both in Volume 4 no. 1. In his editorial to that issue, Michael Schmidt writes of the necessity of understanding the 'wider context' of poetry and of the importance of the artist's understanding 'the frontiers of his freedom of action and expression'. It is an understanding that he and his magazine have always sought.

Boat

GABRIEL JOSIPOVICI

Packed like sardines, yet upright in their seats, eyes fixed firmly ahead.

Where are they going? To the afterlife? To conquer a neighbouring country? To sell and to buy?

The beautiful symmetry of the steersman at the stern, holding the enormous primitive rudder, facing the crew. The pronounced *curve* of the boat, the men in the middle, at the lowest point.

They stare straight ahead, but their backs are to their goal – they are rowers, after all.

Not a boat but the model of a boat, no more than half a metre long.

Why does it move me so much? When I first saw it, in the Egyptian section of the refurbished Ashmolean Museum in Oxford, and now on the card I purchased as I left and which I look at as I write?

Moves me more than would a life-size boat, a real boat, in a real river.

Is it the sense of the men crowded into that small space as a community, silently and purposefully moving in their own time yet in a timeless present, without doubts, without thoughts, plying their oars?

Buried in the sands of Beni Hassan, half way along the Nile between Lower and Upper Egypt. To emerge again in the last century and eventually end up in the Ashmolean.

I am not interested in Egyptian Archaeology. Or in Ancient Egyptian naval technology. I am not 'interested' in this boat. It moves me. The silence of these men moves me. It speaks to me. Let me try and make its quiet voice heard.

Footnote to a larger story

BARRY WOOD

I first heard tell of Michael Schmidt in the summer of 1971. My wife, Patricia, and I had ben invited to tea by Edgell and Beatrix Rickword. It was a hot day, Tricia was six months pregnant, and we travelled by bus from Colchester via Eight Ash Green to the Rickwords' weekend retreat in Halstead, on the Essex/Suffolk border. We were treated to scones and fresh strawberries and made to feel very welcome by them both. As I remember, the conversation was fairly wide-ranging but mainly about poetry. Edgell was intrigued by my interest in Hugh MacDiarmid and particularly pleased by Tricia's admiration for his poetry. In the course of the conversation, she asked about the possibility of a Collected Poems to take the place of the 1947 Bodley Head and 1970 Enitharmon volumes which were essentially selections. Edgell replied with unusual enthusiasm for a reputedly taciturn man that there was 'a young chap in Oxford called Michael Schmidt' who apparently had plans to set up a new press and wanted to publish ER's collected poems and a collection of his essays.

A footnote? Well yes. At any rate, a glimpse into the beginning of an extraordinary adventure in the publication of poetry which – driven by the energy, commitment and extraordinary catholicity of judgement, taste and insight of its originator – resulted in the continuing achievements of the Carcanet Press and *PNR*.

The Poet Himself: on Talking to Stanley on the Telephone

NEIL ASTLEY

Age has not diminished Michael Schmidt's boyish wonder at the world but rather made his bemused questioning of the foibles of its fickle folk all the merrier and more poignant. These are also poems of self questioning, with Schmidt talking not just to Stanley Moss on the phone at night but engaging with the past (himself as a boy) while addressing himself in the present (still a boy at heart). They are wry, playful monologues puzzling over what can only be unpacked, or more often left equivocal, in the poem itself, for, as he writes, 'tone is part of content, part of content', 'content' being both the poem's subject and its pleasing resolution. Reading this book, we find ourselves in the stimulating company of a poet-conversationalist *par excellence*, listening to what might feel addressed to us while eavesdropping on what is clearly not.

Chat GPT Reflects on the Legacy of Michael Schmidt and *PN Review*

GREG O'BRIEN

Characters:
William Empson, English literary critic and poet
Robert Graves, British poet, historical novelist, and critic

Setting: A pub in London

Scene: (William Empson and Robert Graves sit at a table in a pub. They are drinking pints of ale and smoking pipes.)

Empson: (taking a sip of his ale) Have you heard about Michael Schmidt's anniversary?

Graves: (looking up from his pipe) Anniversary of what?
Empson: Of *PN Review*. It's been fifty years since he founded the journal.
Graves: (nodding) Ah yes, I remember when it first came out. It was a breath of fresh air in the literary world.
Empson: (smiling) Indeed. Michael has done a remarkable job of keeping it going all these years.
Graves: (smiling) He certainly has. I remember some of the early issues – there was such a range of voices and ideas, from all over the world.
Empson: (nodding) Yes, and that's still true today. He's managed to keep *PN Review* relevant and interesting,

despite all the changes in the literary world.

Graves: (thoughtful) It's really quite an achievement. And he's published some remarkable writers over the years.

Empson: (smiling) Yes, I remember reading some of your work in *PN Review,* Robert.

Graves: (laughing) Yes, and you had some things to say about it, if I recall.

Empson: (smiling) Of course, that's what critics do.

Graves: (nodding) Indeed. But it's not just the big names that Michael has published. He's always been interested in discovering new voices and giving them a platform.

Empson: (smiling) Yes, that's one of the things that's made *PN Review* so important over the years. It's been a real incubator for new talent.

Graves: (nodding) And he's always been very open-minded about different kinds of writing. Poetry, fiction, essays – he's willing to publish anything that's good.

Empson: (smiling) And that's why *PN Review* has had such a wide appeal over the years. It's a place where people can go to find something interesting and challenging to read.

Graves: (nodding) And that's a real testament to Michael's vision and hard work. He's done something really remarkable with *PN Review*.

Empson: (raising his glass) Here's to Michael and *PN Review* – may they continue to thrive for many more years to come.

Edith Sitwell's Jacket

(for Michael Schmidt)

THOMAS McCARTHY

We placed our bid on an unexpected green jacket
During lockdown at the Sacheverell sale –
One of Edith's poetry-reading outfits, all pale
Green buttons; and all the fabric beautifully cut
By Nina Astier of Chelsea. We had imagined
A surprise presentation to Martina, a poet's coat
For her to wear on the London reading circuit.
Despite our double-bid some other poetry fiend
Beat us to the greeny prize. Yet the thought
Of clothing a fellow poet in diamante and silk
Is with you still: that publishing instinct
To glorify another loyal Carcanet name
With something valuable and lovely. From Ilk-
ley to Mount Parnassus, such yearnings do remain.

Discoveries

STAV POLEG

Over the years, I have found *PNR* to be the most essential read – not only as a source of inspiration or finding new favourite poets, but also as a vital learning resource. To give but one example – reading *PNR*, and in particular the editorial for *PNR 247*, sent me looking for Marjorie Perloff's works, finding among them *Wittgenstein's Ladder*. It was one of those most wonderful literary domino effects: reading *PNR* led to reading Perloff which led to Wittgenstein's *Philosophical Investigations*, a book I found myself delving into for months on end. As for my own writing, when Michael suggested that I write a short essay about the experience of creating in English as a foreign language, I was not sure what to do. Until that point, I never thought this would be a subject of any interest and I had absolutely no idea what I could possibly write apart from the fact that it was always a challenge. But soon after I started working on the essay, I found the process of writing it to be entirely unexpected. It felt as if I was experimenting with language in an unfamiliar way, constantly discovering new material while trying to make sense of the past. I would not have embarked on it without the encouragement from Michael, and I will be forever grateful for his editorial insight and intuition!

Étude

JOHN R. LEE

and we try to *see* Irina, in Kyiv,

playing Chopin on an ash-covered piano
in the bombed-out debris of her house.

What do we *see*? What does it mean?
What epiphany under that apocalypse?
What imagination confronts unreasoning tyranny

with defiant chords?

Over the darkened streets, shrieking fire –
shattered window-glass underfoot,

denuded rubble of homes,
spectral shapes of hollowed architecture,
tragedy become ordinary far from those cities.

Gymnasium

A.T. BOYLE

Before lockdown he walked every day back and forth to the office. When the keys to Cross Street were made redundant and the doors to a gymnasium next to home barred too, this long-time editor of *PNR* was never going to stand still.

But let us row back a little.

Michael Schmidt in the editorial for summer 2020's *PNR* 254 recalls another editor's discovery. When preparing 'Jubilee in Letters' in 2019 to celebrate Carcanet's half century of book publishing, Robyn Marsack noticed that archive correspondence about Eavan Boland was brief, whereas this poet wrote 'with feeling and generosity' about others' work. Michael notes that Boland's influence extended far beyond the forty-seven contributions 'made in her own voice'. And that he 'cannot say how many times she is present by suggestion or simply by her example, which persists'.

The persistent space Michael has made for an array of voices that have come and gone and come again in a hemi-century of *PNR* since 1973 – whether long or short or shaped form poem, feature, review, or letter – is capacious. And we must not forget the voices that have been engendered through these varied presentations.

Whenever I read Michael's words I hear the undulations and emphases of his own voice even as he is quoting other voices. I sense the imbued emotions and politics, an always bubbling energy in that love of the variety of poetic perspectives. I enjoy the givens of his sharp wit. Michael is in the room with me, presenting to me directly the truest evaluations he can muster of the ideas he espouses and those he diverges from.

Six months following *PNR* 254, the first Covid lockdown hit Manchester and everywhere else. Michael's response? Undiminished energy. The machinery of press must still be attended to. There are books, computers, photocopier, a franking machine which for a year's stretch will only know the touch of his fingers. There will be nothing to publish if the correspondence and imaginative activities pause. The machinery of words will not function without constant scrutiny, encouragement, input, energy.

As we know with Michael, disappointing news is blasted with pithy resolution and upbeat elision. Barred from Cross Street and the local gymnasium, Michael informed me he was now running up and down the apartment block stairs. The number of times each stair must encounter his trotting feet had been carefully calculated to match that daily walk to the office. A new structure was already in place. No hassle. We laughed. Good idea. Resilience. Irrepressibility. A familiar back-up battery that will never go lazy.

Geographic strictures will not inhibit this peripatetic *PNR* editor who has ably run a gymnasium for fifty years with the help of sage literary advisors and skilled colleagues.

Just imagine if Michael did ever choose dotage – doubtful – but, I can see him watching over a 'real' Modernist gym. Indulgent scrutiny will be palpable and active in that sporty space. Like any good trainer he will continue to elucidate true talent wherever he finds it. He will hold on to it.

Unlike Aristotle in 323 BC, in 2023 AD Mr Schmidt will not be leaving the city where he made his home. Instead, I hear: leg curl, leg press, cable triceps, arm row, keep the energy up!

There he sits, persisting by example, calling out incisive encouragement here and there from an elevated corner stool. How could we not all make our best endeavours in response?

¡Que Viva Mexico!

IAIN BAMFORTH

Keep your passport for 'the surrealist place par excellence' –
its chaos-politics a measure of its attractiveness
for artists tamed by Europe. On the 1929 *Variétés* world map
it dominates the States: no government and hardly a state to call its own
but every year it mounts the Theatre of Cruelty
and the Conquest happens all over again and guts you where you sit.
Here's where Eisenstein came to instruct himself
in the revolutionary power of montage. An upturned U means
class oppression. A weaving-motif is a grammar lesson.
Mesoamerica, the land for artists who need to say No.

So pin your poems on the cactus sprouting by the porch,
the bristly spines of succulent knowledge,
and leave a set of directions for our peyote specialist, Ambrose Bierce,
still disappearing into the Aztec calendar –
on his shoulder the black and red oconenetl bird
identified in Tlaxcala and of reputedly hallucinogenic flesh.

Follow them out of the dark and into the white-washed house.

50 Not Out

JAMES KEERY

Fifty not out – fifty years, not fifty numbers! *PN Review* amazed me when I first got my hands on a copy. Sixty double-columned pages – I remember turning them in disbelief – it was No. 27, which is coming apart as I turn them now, with the beautiful cover lettering – PN REVIEW and 27 in inch-high green bold separated by one of three paragraphs of names and titles in red – and on the back cover, the other way round – what have we here? It was the first poetry magazine I came across – restricted to Peter Porter's monthly round-up in the *Observer* – via Ashbery's *As We Know* – another double-columned treasure-trove. *PN Review* and Carcanet have meant the world to me ever since. *A Various Art*, *A Whole Bauble*, *Collected Poems* by Lynette Roberts, Séan Rafferty and it was unwise to begin a list because where would it end?

In *Poetry (London)* No. 7, my other editorial hero, Tambimuttu, reflects, with Eliot at Faber and Faber in mind, on the 'commercial limits to the poetry list a publisher can carry': 'A man of perception at a publishing house prints a few poets... He also publishes subsequent volumes of the poets, but is now unable, owing to commercial limits, (and his just behaviour...) to encourage new poets... as they "arrive"'. Carcanet has somehow defied gravity in publishing first and subsequent collections by ever more 'new poets as they arrive' – and time and again someone apparently long gone pops up with a resplendent *Collected Poems*.

How their editor has managed without a pen-drive of

extra brain-capacity and Tardis hours in the middle of the night I cannot imagine. I know he's a quick study, and thinks nothing of knocking out a biography of the novel – but how quickly *can* you read *poetry*? It stubbornly insists on being read a word at a time, yielding nothing whatever to a skim or a scan. Not that you have to eat the whole ox – but one of the things I like best about Michael as an editor is that there's no one between him and his mail. I used to get rejections from P. Heaton, the usual chucker-out who knows the kind of thing the editor wants and saves him the trouble of reading the rest – only to learn that it was Michael all along, saving his own signature for acceptances. And he doesn't just *publish* a collection – I remember the process, from ticks on a long-list of poems to an argument about the spelling of the word 'wigeon', which I lost, which is why it has a bloody 'd' in it. No, it's fine, I've moved on – and I think I pretty much went with the ticks – taking the direct hit on the 'sinless confessional epics' – not that I wasn't bothered, but just because I'd come to trust his judgement. I still do.

For *PN Review*

SAM ADAMS

It must have been in 1973 that Meic Stephens, then Literature Director at the Welsh Arts Council, was approached by a Manchester-based publisher seeking an editor for an anthology of Anglo-Welsh poetry he proposed to add to his list. This was unprecedented, a shock: Meic had devoted a good deal of office time fruitlessly endeavouring to persuade publishers in England to take an interest in writing from Wales. The project landed in my lap, for which I was and remain extremely grateful. *Ten Anglo-Welsh Poets*, which took its place alongside similar collections from Ireland, Scotland and America, was my introduction to Carcanet, and of course to Michael Schmidt and *PN Review*. The magazine was an eye-opener. I had assisted Meic, founding editor (in 1965) of the quarterly *Poetry Wales,* by looking after the reviews section, and knew that, though not unwelcoming to 'outsiders', it considered its primary duty to serve Welsh writers and our bilingual reading public. And here was a younger, elegant periodical out of a city with a population then very similar in size to that of Wales, which had a world-wide catchment of contributors and readers. Nor did it deal exclusively in English-language literature: poetry in translation featured frequently along with critical studies, literary lore and news of writers and writing from around the globe. Clearly, its editor possessed a breadth of vision and a generous spirit of intellectual goodwill to match the fearsome resources of energy needed to keep up a bi-monthly production and an academic day job – not to mention a burgeoning press, volumes of his own poems and fiction, and authorship of compendious studies of the history of poetry and the novel. So far as I can make out, Michael first nodded through my review of some Anglo-Welsh texts in *PNR* 28, 1986 and there were other odds and ends to keep up the connection before my first 'Letter from Wales' came a decade later. *PNR* 109, that was a turning point: with time on my hands, I had at last a reason to write, a living subject and someone to write for. I have shelves loaded with every issue published since, a treasured archive. Congratulations on *PNR*'s fiftieth and warmest good wishes to all concerned.

To Glasgow

SHERI BENNING

I moved to Glasgow in late February 2008 entirely motivated by my desire to study with Michael. I recall meeting with him in his attic office at the university, how his generous conversation filled me with a hovering sense of potential, a lightness like the spring sun that streamed through his window. I recall laughter, mine on occasion so uproarious that once an administrator in the next office requested that the Canadian please quiet down. Fair enough: my laugh, shaped by vast prairie horizons, was made irrepressible by Michael's eye-twinkling wit.

When Michael left the University of Glasgow, I would take the early morning train to Manchester to meet with him at Carcanet's offices, returning to Glasgow that same evening. I loved these journeys, the anticipation for our chats, and then, on the ride home, a renewed inspiration for the work. In the hemmed-in privacy of a cramped train carriage, the darkening sky, I read collections that Michael had pressed into my hands before my departure: Judith Wright, Les Murray, Eavan Boland, Bridget Pegeen Kelly. I was writing about my natal home, a marginal farm in central Saskatchewan, and Michael was right: these poets, along with the many others he's suggested over the years, have helped my home-place come into clearer view.

In a recent editorial for the *PN Review*, Michael writes that poetry reading is collaborative, that '[c]ollaboration is basic to the art itself'. I sometimes wrote poems on the train ride home from Manchester, Michael's conversation in mind. 'A poem can come to know more than its poet did', Michael writes in the same editorial. Now, when I look back on this work, I recognize something bravely beheld, necessary insight that was made possible by Michael's voice. To say I'm grateful – for his friendship, his writing, his curation – is not enough.

*

To Glasgow

Standing on the platform, Manchester Victoria,
waiting for the after supper train. Home,
to Glasgow.

Spring sky, bruised fruit. Pigeons in eaves.
Rain-bloated newsprint, overripe peonies
that lined the porch at the farm,
long sold.

A breeze lifts my hair, sweat of my nape,
a train, not mine, shoots past. Diesel,
smoke from the burn barrel at dusk,
the farm again,

dew on bluestem, my body, my breath. My face
in the windows of passing cars. *I am. I am.*

There is no going back.

Der Kleiber: *Eurasian Nuthatch*

(*Sitta europaea*)

SUJATA BHATT

...What's the littlest thing
  You can spin a poem out of...?
    – Michael Schmidt

Over here there are enough trees
to make us feel sheltered.

We hear it first, a loud song:
the clear notes so sharp, it makes us stop.
But there is no fear we think, no pain.
When we look up, we see the bird:
tiny, unlikely.
You say it's the only bird
that can descend trees headfirst.
The bird hovers. I say it might fly away.
This one has a blue-grey upper body
and orange-peach underparts.

We watch it climb higher and forage.
And then we hear it sing again.
We watch, not wanting to disturb it.
And yet, not wanting to leave.
There we stand, looking up, when suddenly
the bird moves down the tree, headfirst.

'...
Of luring words like flocks of birds
To settle bookwards, readerwards
And oh – why not – eternitywards!'

Edwin Morgan 'I ought to write this in Nahuatl'

Image: Mary Griffiths, 'Manchester Cathedral
from the Corn Exchange' (2023). Photo © Michael Pollard.

A Garden

JAMES WOMACK

And then there's the house I walk past every morning on my way to nursery. I don't quite know how to read it: when we first moved into the street I thought it was a bourgeois experiment: large outwards-facing garden left to rewild. Yorkshire fog, cocksfoot, foxtail: grasses growing in clumps and tourbillons so that by the end of summer it was less a garden and more a series of tiny turtle-back islands.

Now, I'm not so sure it is a deliberate experiment. The grass rises and falls, a year-long breath. I have never seen anyone enter or leave the house. The garden sometimes looks slightly sinister: in early summer I thought *this grass is tall enough to hide a body*. But also, with the spring come round again, astonishing deep red tulips and dole queues of grape hyacinths the whole length of the back wall.

You see the metaphor working, almost.

PNR has always known the difference between an editor and a gardener. On my computer I have tedious back-and-forth archives, blood-pressure arguments with little-magazine Le Nôtres, all of them convinced that every evanescent quarterly issue has to be as trimmed and prinked as the parks at Versailles (and terrified to the tips of their full-bottom wigs of upsetting this season's Sun King). I also have a few laconic messages exchanged with Michael: 'Can I ...?' 'Yes', or, rarely, 'No'.

This is how an editor should work. It's not rewilding: *PNR* is not desperately trying to reintroduce the beaver. But it's not neglect, either: the ground has been raked and sown and now the editor can stand back and see how, over time, the prepared space starts to tell its own story. The wild hawthorn flourishes. The undergrowth grows thick.

Carcanet Towers

LAURA SCOTT

There's a pen and ink sketch somewhere of Alliance House, where Carcanet has its office – Carcanet Towers, as I gather it's called. I can't find the drawing anywhere now, so of course it glows in my head as a thing of beauty. I remember the impressive facade, the mullioned windows, the grandness of scale and the capacious interior

it implied. Somewhere inside that building I liked to imagine the oak-panelled headquarters of *PNR*, where dozens of people bustle around piles of poems.

I liked the picture because even if that's a fantasy, it's a manifestation of what's really distinctive about *PNR*: the ambition, the rangey catholic tastes, the internationalism, the way it's the opposite of parochial. I wanted to be in there, inside that splendid building, roaming its rooms.

At least, that's what I thought I wanted, but this desire changed into something else as soon as I got a response from Michael to one of my poems. It wasn't that I didn't care any more, it was rather that once the conversation started, the possibilities of extending it and opening it up seemed more interesting than simply getting in the door. I'd sent a sort of sonnet where the move in the middle was not so much a turn as a lurch; it had to be like that. I got an email back from Michael: 'I cannot quite get, though I think I instinctively follow without being able to see how, the transition. Tell me how it works.' Did that mean my poem had been accepted or not? Wrong question.

In fact I don't think I've ever got a poem into *PNR* without an exchange of this kind. At first, I didn't realise how unusual this was, and now, I fear, I rather take it for granted. But I shouldn't, because it is a wonderful thing: an editor who can't stop teaching, giving, stirring it up. An email from Michael is always fun, the voice that speaks in it is both amused and amusing, never commonplace. Recently a poem of mine got stuck in the in-tray at Carcanet Towers, and by the time it emerged it had already been accepted by another magazine. There's nothing wrong with the other magazine, but I was still a bit disappointed. More than I wanted to see the poem in print, I wanted to hear how Michael read it.

STEPHEN RAW

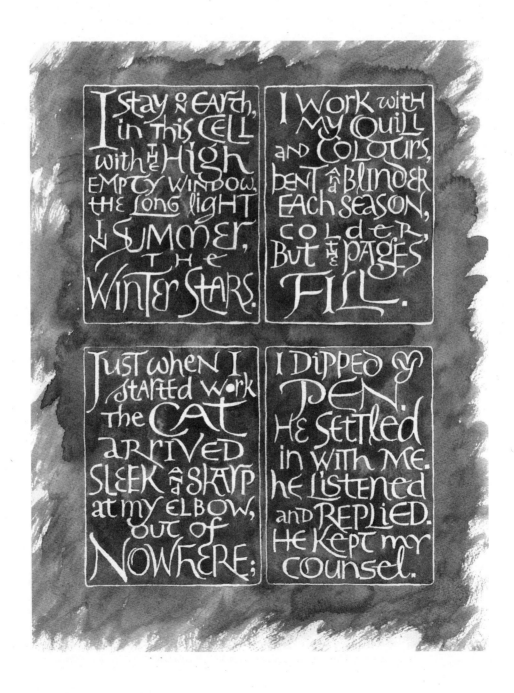

'We have to get this into the next issue of *PN Review*'

JUDITH WILLSON

When I joined Carcanet as managing editor, I thought I understood how things worked. A book publisher. They publish a magazine as well. I had worked in book publishing, and for many years I had been assistant editor of an academic journal that had made its way to the printer twice a year since the 1950s, a stately ship with a cargo of footnotes. It was a shock to discover that *PN Review* was somewhat different. It took me months to get to grips with the dynamics of its production schedule. Neil Powell, who had been involved with the magazine for years as proofreader, copyeditor and contributor, talked me through it with the generous, slightly weary, patience of a teacher trying yet again to get a child to understand long division. Grant Shipcott the typesetter talked me through it again – and rescued me on many occasions, creating clarity and order as deadlines came to a rolling boil. Gradually, I came to understand: *PN Review* was not a magazine published *in addition* to books, it was the energy that drove Carcanet itself. The headlong rush of production was the product of Michael's enthusiasms, wanting to share with readers a wonderful new poem, an exciting new poet, a conversation, in their immediacy, before they became fixed into books. And how many poetry magazines include articles about music, art, philosophy, rereadings of forgotten poets ...? Or cartoons, like the eerie little drawings that were used to fill empty spaces – because why not, isn't such multifariousness what makes poetry interesting? Isn't this what matters? It's a great editor who opens a space in this way to enlarge your world. For fifty years Michael has shaped a magazine that is, like its editor, sharp-witted and serious, alive to the world and to the languages that poetry makes from it. Long may both continue to flourish, without ever becoming stately.

Crisis for Cranmer

LORNA GOODISON

Issue # 13 of *PNR*, titled 'Crisis For Cranmer and King James' and dedicated to the Book of Common Prayer, is one that Ted and I often refer to as an example of publication in service to humanity. That is true of almost every issue of *PNR*.

There is no other magazine quite like it for its determination to illuminate whatsoever things are pure and lovely, and to challenge both the comfortable and the contrary in the world of words. Thank you, Michael Schmidt, for the presence of *PNR* in the world lo these fifty years.

Of Machines and the Man

HELEN TOOKEY

For me, as I'm sure for so many other people, *PN Review* has been a doorway opening onto many things. I first met Michael in the early 2000s, when I was newly in Liverpool, working as a freelance editor and also trying to learn about poetry – as a writer, but, necessarily before that, as a reader. Michael needed a proofreader for the magazine and I was lucky enough to get the job. There could have been no better way to learn. The pages of *PN Review* opened up to me to a world of poems and poets, of thinking about poetry and what it can effect – a world of great depth and variety, seriousness and strangeness.

At the same time, of course, there was the very practical business of keeping the show on the road. If a poem is, as William Carlos Williams famously put it, a machine made of words, then a bimonthly poetry magazine is a kind of meta-machine, made of many smaller machines – poems and poets, budgets and deadlines, authors and editors, software, hardware, paper and ink and printing presses and warehouses and postal systems – many of which frequently seem to be pulling in different directions or indeed operating in different space-time continuums. Fixed points, Pole Stars, are hugely to be valued, and for me it was a particular pleasure to work closely with long-time *PN Review* typesetter Grant Shipcott, whose knowledge, reliability, and reassuring presence at the other end of the phone were an essential part of the machinery.

But the designer at the heart of it all, of course, was – is – Michael. I've recently been re-reading John Greening's brilliant long poem 'The Silence' (from his Carcanet collection of the same name), about Jean Sibelius's long struggle to write an eighth symphony; and it strikes me now that Michael's process, in putting together each issue of *PN Review*, must be something like the way a composer writes a symphony, turning over in his head all those different lines and tunes and harmonies and counterpoints, somehow (but how?) keeping it all in play, all in mind, until the shape comes clear, until all the parts fit together and sing. It often seemed like a kind of impossible magician's trick when Michael would emerge from the apparent chaos of his office, bearing a neat stack of paper and the wryly triumphant smile of someone who has managed to *win through*, and announce the next issue, ready for production.

To have shaped and published each issue of *PN Review* for fifty years is an extraordinary achievement, but then Michael is an extraordinary man. Warmest congratulations, Michael, and thank you.

How It Was: Freeze-frame from Archive

MIKE FREEMAN

PNR/Carcanet office, in a Corn Exchange as yet untouched by the IRA and Derrida, circa Michael's *Choosing a Guest: New and Selected Poems*. The Monday morning's fifth hit of instant-coffee against "the thicket growing dark" *[op cit]* but with cherry blossom blowing from the cathedral close, five characters in search of authors, their toy, their dream, their rest.

Michael, cultural commissar's snuff box to hand, seeking the idea of order at key worst phone-calls from Donald D and Charles S in their struggle for his soul.
Robyn shape-shifting authors' *bricolages* into readerly *écriture*.

Pam the Stakhanovite transcribing Michael's midnight dictaphoning.

Peter, acting accountant, deconstructing metafictive aporia, aka royalty statements.

Mike, factotum, deflecting *Angst*-soaked calls from Elizabeth, Christine, Ian – no names, no pack drill.

Stacked between xerox and light-box, the outgoing review copies, the incoming lava flow of unsolicited mss pending politburo scrutiny - *sunt lacrimae rerum*.

Reviews

Sisterhood

Louise Glück, *Marigold and Rose* (Carcanet) £12.99
Reviewed by Paul Franz

Marigold and Rose is Louise Glück's second book to appear since she won the Nobel Prize in October 2020 and her first to bear the designation 'A Fiction'. Neither a novel nor a short story, it is identified in the publicity materials, plausibly enough, as a 'fable'. That term has the advantage of having been favoured by Glück in the past: her *Poems 1962–2012* contains five 'Fables' (not to mention an extensive set of 'Parables'). Yet such poems are not 'fables' in the strict sense – that is, stories 'in which animals substituted for people', to adopt the description of the alphabet book that Marigold, one of the infant protagonists of Glück's new 'fiction', is spotted reading in its opening pages, and which her twin sister Rose, 'a social being', detests. Instead, Glück's fables and parables are what we might call interpretive genres: short narratives, akin to dream, with an enigmatic significance. What then is the significance of *Marigold and Rose*?

Its subject is the infants' first year. Its episodes include: sitting in the garden, learning to climb stairs, imagining their mother's childhood, learning to use a cup and spoon, enduring the death of a grandmother and (by occasion) adults' euphemism and lies, coming to apprehend Mother and Father as distinct people, celebrating a first birthday party. Beneath this changing surface, however, flows its genuine subject: the twins' natures as individuals and how each is shaped or revealed by the other, and by the other's relation to the world. That they cannot talk yet is no great obstacle. *Marigold and Rose* is, after all, also a pastoral – and not just because of its protagonists' floral names. As much as any pastoral discussed by William Empson, its work is one of 'putting the complex into the simple'. And, like many an eclogue, it centres on a contest – albeit a somewhat one-sided one. (Marigold, unlike Rose, is 'writing a book', despite the fact that she can't yet actually read.)

'When I was a small child', Glück declared in her Nobel Lecture, 'I staged a competition in my head, a contest to decide the greatest poem in the world. There were two finalists: Blake's "The Little Black Boy" and Stephen Foster's "Swanee River".' In the fall of 2020, this choice of objects – an antislavery poem of complex racial politics and a minstrel song of yearning for the Old South – was seen as a singularly poor one, though, of course, Glück did not present these first attachments as having been chosen, exactly. Blake's poem was the winner, though Glück later 'realized' that the two poems had something in common, in that both featured 'the solitary human voice, raised in lament and longing'.

Repulsion by 'social' life and its values is a constant in Glück's writing. But her alternative to the 'social' is not the self in sublime isolation. Instead, she was drawn to 'the poets in whose work I played, as the elected listener, a crucial role. Intimate, seductive, often furtive or clandestine.' Her poetry, as Helen Vendler once observed, is 'post-psychoanalytic'. Its arena is the family, scene of primordial attachments and conflicts. (Glück's sister Tereze, herself a writer and a corporate executive, died in 2018; a third sister died in infancy.) If the Nobel forced this least public of poets to articulate the value of the private in public terms, her latest work might seem like a strong reversion to the private. It would be truer, though, to see it as restaging – within the seemingly neutral sphere of infancy – an abiding conflict of values.

Coincidentally or not, *Marigold and Rose* is one of several recent works of prose fiction – think of books by Elena Ferrante, Yiyun Li and Sheila Heti, among others – to present a conflict between female protagonists who are typically close, often childhood, friends. Much as in the 'agon' the critic Jonathan Baskin has identified in Heti's work, one axis of conflict in *Marigold and Rose* is over how to interpret the agon itself. Do its alternatives represent a choice? Or are they, rather, irreducibly opposite natures? When Rose mentally exhorts Marigold to 'swell the ranks', she makes the typical assumption of the 'social' characters in these works, that non-participation is a choice. For the artists, however, it is an existential decision. Their only true choice is whether to espouse or betray their own calling.

When Heti's novel *Pure Colour* (2022) asserts, fancifully, that different human types are born from different 'eggs', it signals its commitment to the artist's view. The more ambiguous *Marigold and Rose* follows the principle of *nomen est omen*. 'Rose was perennial', we read (that is, singular, the cynosure of every eye), while 'Marigold was annual' (that is, multiple, nomadic, lacking in stable identity). Whether these names – presumably conferred by the infants' parents – are the makers or the revealers of their natures we are not told. What is certain is that the twins grow into them. Marigold's multiplicity is tenacious.

Yet if the conflict in *Marigold and Rose* resonates with contemporary prose fiction, it also takes up Glück's abiding interest in unbalanced pairs. The title poem of *The Triumph of Achilles* (1985) tells of the friendship between the Greek hero, 'who was nearly a god', and Patroclus, who 'resembled him; they wore / the same armor' – and was hence, in a manner of speaking, his twin. 'Always in these friendships', the poem declared, 'one serves the other, one is lesser than the other: / the hierarchy is always apparent.' While the infant world of *Marigold and Rose* appears remote from that of Homeric epic, the distance is not so great as might be supposed – and not just because of the notorious petulance of the epic heroes. Who is to be the centre of attention, whose life will be held worthy of esteem, whose account of the world and of the mind is to have authority: such are the stakes in a struggle that reveals itself, increasingly, as asymmetric.

To the world, the gregarious Rose appears triumphant, and Marigold herself at times feels her difference from her sister as a deficiency. And yet a change is brewing. In the long run, the battle favours Marigold – and Rose knows it. Indeed, there is in Rose's heart of hearts 'a deep vein of humility, born, she later felt, of her love for her sister, a reverence slightly tinged with awe, as though to Rose Marigold was a kind of prophet or holy figure'. The qualification here – 'she later felt' – is typical of the book's reluctance to offer an authoritative pronouncements unmediated by the twins' own perceptions. At the same time, it introduces a skeptical note, and one that is hardly more favourable to Rose than, one senses, her 'reverence' for her sister is, in the narrator's eyes, creditable.

If this unrequited adoration, so unexpected in its reversal of the apparent pecking order of the sisters, recalls the 'hierarchy' of Achilles and Patroclus, it also – in its dramatic irony, its invitation to look behind Rose's account of her own feelings – marks one of several moments in which *Marigold and Rose* recalls the problematic dyad in 'The Little Black Boy' of Blake. For many modern readers, Blake's poem dramatizes a psychic injury stemming from (in this case racial) subordination; it shows how the self-consciousness of the member of the subjugated group can be warped by its reflection through the categories of the dominant. This is certainly how Glück reads the poem in her Nobel speech, and part of what makes it 'heartbreaking and also deeply political'.

Yet *Marigold and Rose*, by forgoing social determinants, also forgoes the political charge. (When Rose asserts her own superior age and wisdom – she was born first – her facetious appeal to primogeniture falls on deaf ears.) The book vigorously affirms Marigold over her sister. This is not to say it does so without qualification or remainder. (Rose may be right, for instance, that she understands Marigold 'much better than she understands me', even if Rose barely understands Marigold at all.) Yet whom the book favours is never in doubt – least of all towards the end, when we find a startling intrusion of the narrator's voice. In the last chapter, Rose, having greatly enjoyed the twins' first birthday party, reflects that Marigold should end her book with it: 'It would even, she thought to herself, make a nice ending. End on a bright note, she thought.' The narrator then twists the knife: 'as though that were a good or even a possible thing'.

But rejecting happy endings does not mean simply affirming the power of time. Within *Marigold and Rose*'s sprightly narrative of growth, of challenges encountered and surmounted, there runs a deeper strain that rejects the dominance of what merely occurs – and, perhaps, what merely happens to dominate. 'Marigold was absorbed in her book', the opening sentence tells us, 'she had gotten as far as the *V*.' The alphabet is not a narrative, of course; its arbitrary sequence is there to be mastered and recombined. Life, though lived forward, is likewise susceptible of being transformed – even if only by the minimal gesture by which Marigold, racing ahead of her own experience, proposes to write what she knows (that is, her parents' lives), then change the names.

For all its lightness and charm, *Marigold and Rose* retains its hard core. The writer-as-infant is both radically dependent and radically free, imprisoned by a resemblance to her worldly sibling that will, as her inner life takes shape, fall away like a snake's skin. 'Everything will disappear', Marigold reflects. 'Still, she thought, I know more words now. She made a list in her head of all the words she knew: Mama, Dada, bear, bee, hat. And both these things would continue happening: everything will disappear but I will know more words.' The bitter wisdom of 'The Triumph of Achilles', that 'the legends / cannot be trusted – / their source is the survivor, / the one who has been abandoned', has not been contradicted. The book ends with Marigold abandoned to her task: 'All night she wrote. She wrote and wrote and wrote and wrote.'

Critic at Large

D.J. Taylor, *Critic at Large: Essays and Reviews: 2010–2022* (Shoestring Press) £10
Reviewed by Declan Ryan

D.J. Taylor is such a student of the machinations of Grub Street he even, glancingly, feels obliged to review *this* book, a collection of his pieces for various literary magazines over the past decade. If not offering quite a full diagnosis, he is, at least, unable to 'ignore the faint air of defensiveness that rises over these compilations, born of a suspicion that the book review, as opposed to the critical essay... has a necessarily short shelf-life'. There's truth to that, but luckily the work collected here is, on the whole, something slightly more ambitious than the term 'book review' may initially conjure, not least because the art of the review has changed rather dramatically during Taylor's now three-decades long writing life. Taylor started out, he writes, in the promisingly titled piece 'Why Review Books?' in a period where reviewing was 'becoming a blood sport again': literary coverage was wide and wide-ranging, and critics were allowed, even tacitly expected, to cultivate an air of scepticism, if not outright hostility, towards the offerings being scrutinised. Things have changed a fair bit since those relatively heady days of both space and appetite, however, and, as Taylor mournfully notes of the current 'landscape', 'we inhabit a world in which most books are not so much reviewed as endorsed'.

Taylor's is a more robust approach, as he demonstrates throughout this gathering of articles. A sharp noticer, broadly and deeply read, he is able to look both ways, bringing an air of scrupulous entertainment and historical grounding to the process, remembering that a reader's attention is never a given, and nor is their desire to fork out £15 for a book which critics have wrongly neglected to warn them is a dud. He writes bracingly, with authority, but also with a fluid attentiveness to the memorable phrase; on Rushdie-land 'that brightly burnished fakir's bazaar where stories run riot on all sides, where horizon-hugging baroque alternates with finicking close-up rococo', while Alan Bennett is 'above all a complainer, an ingrate of... indefatigable persistence' dishing out 'backward-looking radicalism'. He is very good at this sort of disabused observation, as he is on the late Brian Sewell: 'One should always be suspicious of people who make claims of outsider status, if only because it usually takes an insider to be in a position to make them'.

Status, and class, are preoccupations for Taylor, and one of the great strengths of the work gathered here is its awareness of these driving forces, and its immersion in the motivations and frustrations of characters in books concerned with the crossing of lines, or striving for 'betterment'. At one stage Taylor writes that 'Gissing, it is fair to say, is everywhere in Orwell', and one might say Orwell and his nuanced awareness of British habits, his scrutiny of the desires of ordinary people, functions in a similarly abiding way in Taylor. This, in turn, is based around Taylor's awareness of the history of the British novel and its obsession with social climbing, as a piece on H.G. Wells – another perennial presence – discusses. 'It is not just that social aspirations of any kind are faintly ridiculous, and that no one in their right mind would want to sacrifice the companionship of people of their own social class for dismal little dinners and mock-refined chatter about art... social distinctions are unavoidable because they exist in every section of society'. This sense, that eco-systems of hostility, ambition and thwarted hope exist in every street and village, not just in a few square miles of London, informs Taylor's writing on everything from the novels of early twentieth-century social realism to a close-reading of the Beatles.

A steeliness and refreshing degree of class consciousness, and the knock-on effects it can have within fictional plots and writers' lives, comes to characterise Taylor's writing. He has his occasional tic – the phrase *apologia pro vita sua* crops up more regularly than it might in everyday conversation – and he isn't above doing a little of what he discovers in Orwell, on occasion, being 'in hot pursuit of... the small but irresistible matter of his bygone self' when discussing the lost land of combative critical culture. One senses a nostalgia not only for the period in which he came of age but for the dreamed of, ink-spattered world of Gissing, Connolly, Gross and other heroes. He does note, in 'Why Review Books?', his growing awareness that the idea of laying down the law, or being blind to one's own prejudices, feels a less certain or even desirable position from our current vantage point. That said, one can't help wishing with him for the return of a little more of the blood sport aspect, of the fulsome brand of public reaction Taylor discusses and practices, in our current climate of smiling encouragement masquerading as criticism.

Queering the Green

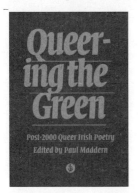

Paul Maddern, editor, *Queering the Green: Post-2000 Queer Irish Poetry* (The Lifeboat Press) £15
Reviewed by Joe Carrick-Varty

Truth be told, I've always found poetry anthologies a little impenetrable. Is that bad? Am I wrong to feel this way? As a mode of poetry publishing, the anthology certainly makes a lot of sense. The anthology does what the magazine does, but on a larger scale, and often with a curated, pre-packaged theme. Be it the prose poem or haiku, be it poems about rivers or climate change, there's just more of everything; more pages, more poets, more poems, which, on paper, sounds great. In today's culture we're always asking for more... more bang for your buck, more meat on the bone. But why, then, do poetry anthologies leave me cold? I can happily guzzle a poetry magazine, containing three-ish poems per poet, and feel tantalisingly nourished enough to, perhaps, having loved a particular poem, hop online to buy the book (if only to be disappointed by said book a week later). Maybe it's the brevity of each poet's carved space, no one shouting too loudly within the chorus of voices. Or maybe it's my attention span, which is more at ease when purveying less than more. Either way, it's safe to say I've never had that feeling of nourishment from a poetry anthology... until now.

In the introduction to *Queering the Green: Post-2000 Queer Irish Poetry*, the anthology's editor Paul Maddern writes: 'It is my belief that Irish identity is being radically reconfigured; what constitutes 'Irishness' is up for debate as never before in recent times – and queer Irish poets are leading the way in asking how that identity is to be redrawn in the twenty-first century.'

Yes please! You had me at 'radically reconfigured'. Such alliterative newness! Such sumptuous possibility! This is, perhaps, a poetry anthology for me...

Maddern goes on to speak of the landscape of Irishness (both physical and metaphorical), with obvious focus on Irish poetry, which, for a long time, has remained somewhat of a robust, fixed idea within the wider cultural consciousness. Landscape (we'll come back to landscape), it turns out, will be a central theme across the anthology's pages.

When asked what Irish poetry is, most people (and I'm generalising here, but humour me) might think of Seamus Heaney, of that echelon of white, straight, cis male poet speaking towards a rural, domestic kind of Irishness. As someone born out of the Irish diaspora (my family were economic migrants who emigrated from Dublin to Coventry in the fifties and sixties), I've always struggled with the version of Irishness I read in poems. That Irishness, for all its wonderful poetry, isn't, and never has been, the Irishness I know.

The poems in *Queering the Green* feel like an Irishness I know. And reading those poems feels like breathing one sustained, collective sigh of relief. The moment when queer bodies are seen, and see themselves, within the green landscape of Ireland... and the contours are redrawn, the greenness reconfigured...

So, landscape...

Padraig Regan's remarkable poem 'Salt Island' prefaces the anthology. This poem is as much a rejection (and redemption) of the Irish landscape as it is a recasting of what it means to be Irish: 'I wanted to make a gothic of it all', the trees and the slope and 'the scrap of wool where a sheep had rubbed / a flank against a tree' – all gothic! And a speaker ruining the mood, wanting ice cream: 'I walked over / the hill with my kilt flapping / & thought / wow! all this for me?' To be the landscape but also to be the weather falling on the landscape, to be 'the cloud-quilt which was then breaking up'. But it's kind of heart-breaking, this poem. The speaker, scrolling through photos a week later, sees that 'my red tartan / clashed with the grass so perfectly / I wondered if I intended to be the punctum, / the little rip in the surface'. Oof indeed.

'Salt Island' made me think of that scene in *The Lion King* where Simba and Mufasa purvey the Pride Lands, only in reverse: a kind of queer Irish reversal in which, instead of being told which part of the horizon they own, the speaker, without any boomy-voiced bestower, tries on the landscape like a sequined dress or a pair of spangled boots, squinting, twizzling around, thinking: 'It is too / early to tell if I've succeeded'.

On we go with landscape...

Eva Griffin's poem 'When you type Ganymede into Google it asks' takes an astronomical approach to landscape, forgetting the historical landscape of this planet (this island) 'in favour of bigger moons'. Greenness is, in a sense, forgotten too, the 'Sheep left grazing / in the boyish grass; green and the following wind'. There's a kind of meandering, wandering off in this poem which I love. It's a subtle rejection of traditional modes of greenness, which means it almost isn't a rejection at all, but a natural, organic forgetting, which, by the end of the poem, lands the speaker 'atop / the widest ring of Saturn... one hand reaching for / the tilt of Aquarius, the other hiding my thirsty mouth.'

Annemarie Ní Churreáin's poem 'Border' brings landscape into the body: 'At first I knew nothing of the border / or that I was being divided'. The poem's scale oscillates between 'mountains, valleys, wells' and 'the curves of shoulders... hems of hair that sweep towards the sun'. Here, the very idea of nationhood is reimagined, internalised within a body... the body of Ireland cut in two, its speaker 'divided // from my own kind'. I always enjoy poems that make me think about the definite article of things. I'm writing now about a body, a speaker's body, which, it turns out, is also the living, breathing body of Ireland, with its border sliced clean through. I don't know, there's something compelling about this approach to discourse on the Border; it's a subtle yet physical approach to a huge topic, asking the question: What does it mean for a country to become a body?

Mícheál McCann's poem 'Hook-up' reflects and refracts Ireland's greenness through the green circle of someone's status on Grindr: 'I want to reach around / the green circle... that lets me know they're the same as me'. Seeking connection at 1:38am on a Wednesday, the speaker longs to cross 'this pitch-black Donegal landscape... [where] mystery insects buzz... and ewes rest / under trees'. There's certainly a nod towards a rural, poetic, Irish landscape here, which is quickly recast, as queer bodies enter the fray, not touching exactly, 'we wouldn't touch', but touched by the moon in such haunting holiness:

content instead to watch new lambs
make their way through the darkness
to their mothers, in complete, holy silence.

The poems in *Queering the Green* are, as a collective, impossible to put in a box. Far less a school of voices linked by theme or subject matter, much more a collection of poets writing work that reflects a new kind of Irishness, a poetics that, although engaged with certain aspects of the traditional, is more concerned with redrawing, reconfiguring the landscape.

I'll end this review as I began it, with a quote from editor Paul Maddern's introduction:

every poem is a queering of language; every poetry critic a critic of the queer; every reader of poetry is engaged in a queer act; every performance of poetry is a queer iteration.
But only we are queer.

Myth and Memory

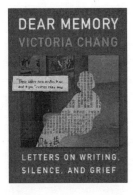

Dear Memory, Victoria Chang, (Milkweed Editions) $25; *Generations: A Memoir*, Lucille Clifton (NYRB Classics) $14.95; *Music, Late and Soon*, Robyn Sarah (Biblioasis) $18.95
Reviewed by Evan Jones

What we know of ancient Homer is myth and supposition, the result of texts and images created centuries after he was meant to have lived. And coming forward in time doesn't mean that we understand someone like Shake-

speare any better. In Ben Jonson, we find that Shakespeare knew 'small Latine and lesse Greeke'. It was Herodotus who guessed that Homer lived 400 years before his *Histories*. Yet the small secrets that sneak out of the work, impossible to verify, are how we hold on to the image of poets – there is Homer in blind Demodocus, performing at the Phaikaian banquet for Odysseus. And – though there are other examples – Autolycus, the roguish peddler of ballads in *The Winter's Tale,* holds great appeal as a stand-in for Shakespeare: 'he haunts / wakes, fairs and bear-baitings'. About right for a bard.

That poets create the myths of their own lives is something we assume they have always done. When a poet's memoir appears, we might look for the tricks and details that help us understand that myth better, filling in background that we traditionally trusted the poems to do, enlightening or even contradicting it. Largely, each of these three books might best be thought of as *Künstlerschriften*: poets on art and life, sharing secrets and ideals.

Victoria Chang's *Dear Memory* posits questions about memory and family history that are impossible to answer decades after an ancestor's passing. Like Anne Carson's *Nox*, the book assembles documents – photos, testimony, affidavits, marriage licenses and house plans – alongside Chang's writing. Her form is epistolary: letters to people she has known, even briefly, and not known. About a grandfather she met once in Taipei, she writes:

I was surprised to read that you had a first wife. I wonder who she was. I wonder what she died of. Now I know I have another aunt, named Yei-pin. I wonder where she was adopted from. I wonder what happened to her parents. Was she from an affair or another marriage? I wonder how she knew your first wife, whether you raised her, what she looks like, whether she is still alive.

Without question marks, all that wondering is declarative, telling us what Chang felt at a distance. When we do get a direct question, the answer is impossible, gossipy, lost.

Loss, Chang seems to argue, cannot be reconstructed, even as fragments allow us to suppose. If the imagination begins to fill in, which it longs to do, which it seems built to do, then this creates fiction – which is the opposite of memoir. Chang pushes in another direction, one geared perhaps towards her poet's intelligence: 'Maybe memories are not to be forgotten but also not exactly to be remembered. Maybe that glorious, lumbering moose that stops us for a moment isn't death after all. Maybe it's memory, which is the exit wound of joy.' That double-edged 'exit wound of joy' is the chief fascination here, in trawling a family history for a sense of coherence in the self. What arrives in the end is a maturity and the acceptance that only an artist can make something of this material.

The 'generations' of Lucille Clifton's memoir, first published in 1976 and now reissued, descend from her great-great-grandmother, called Caroline Donald Sale, born in Dahomey in West Africa in 1822 or 1823 (the text gives different years). Clifton was born in 1936, her father, Samuel Louis Sayles, Sr., in 1902. He was raised by his great-grandmother, Mammy Ca'line, already in her eighties. These relationships between generations are central to Clifton's thinking about identity. Working within the living memory of slavery, she tells us, 'Things don't fall apart. Things hold.' In Clifton, the falconer can hear the falcon. The book is her reconnection to Mammy Ca'line, to the Dahomey women she claims descent from – survivors. 'From Dahomey women' becomes a refrain in the book, though Clifton admits that when she uses the line on her father – as a young woman, justifying dropping out of Howard University after two years – he is 'furious and defensive and sad': 'You don't even know what that is, he frowned at me. You don't even know what it means.'

Generations is Clifton explaining that she does know, though it took her a lifetime and even lifetimes to understand – her father's and her mother's deaths become monuments to that understanding. Her father, in particular, for all his difficulty and disappointment in her – even as Clifton is told she is his favourite – is a source of wisdom for the artist. She recites his lessons throughout the book, not in quotations but in her own speech, her father's voice a part of her: 'When colored people came to Depew they came to be a family. Everybody began to be related in thin ways that last and last. The generations of white folks are just people but the generations of colored folks are families.' These elements inform what Clifton becomes, a line of descent from Mammy Ca'line down to her own six children. The book ends with a list, a family tree of direct descent, where Clifton shows exactly how she comes from the Dahomey women of her understanding, made reality in her writing.

Robyn Sarah's *Music, Late and Soon* revels in her fine eye for precision and detail. Her title alludes to the occasion of the book: thirty-five years after her last piano practice, Sarah returns to the instrument, planning a performance for her sixtieth birthday. She trained as a clarinetist when young and performed with the Montreal Symphony Orchestra, but had left that behind to become a writer in the rush of the creative 1960s.

Music, Late and Soon is a document of the classical music world in Montreal over half a century, of players and teachers, pedagogy and practice, that raises important questions about art. Does the musician create *or* perform? Sarah – poet/maker and musician/performer – struggles to reconcile the two, separates them, wants her developed instincts to inform performance:

> If I liked a poem, I wanted to learn it by heart (people often use this expression to mean 'by rote,' but I really mean by *heart:* not just being able to recite the words from memory, but internalizing the *feelings* they communicate). It's the same with a piece of music: I want to plunge in cold and learn the notes quickly, even if roughly, so I can experience what the whole piece is saying, what it means *emotionally...*

But she admits that 'there are always some passages that defeat me, places where I'm winging it, or faking it.' Sarah internalizes her vision of art's workings and not-workings, the processes she sees herself applying and her unrelenting efforts to understand. This is a book – as indeed are all three – about artistry itself and what makes the artist. Sarah has found a way to think through and mediate her different approaches: she writes them out.

Wry, Chippy, Unapologetic

Don Paterson, *Toy Fights* (Faber) £16.99
Reviewed by Christian Wethered

Toy Fights is a warts-and-all account of a fraught, working-class upbringing in 1970s and 1980s Kirkton (Dundee). The writing is both explicit and distracted – a bit like listening to someone baring their soul in a crowded room – and unafraid to pull a punch or two. It's perhaps closer in tone to the aphorisms, or the coarser *Nil Nil* (1993), than to Paterson's later poems or essays. *Toy Fights*, which comes from a childhood game involving 'twenty minutes of extreme violence without pretext', was supposed to indicate, at the time, 'not serious fights', but really came to mean 'senseless fights' – and has thus defined many of his subsequent conflicts (mainly with God, his father, woke-liberals, drugs and insanity).

There's a lot of anger – partly against his father for dying, and for not earning enough back in the day. This book was originally supposed to be written *for* his father about their shared love of music – but when his father died it morphed into a memoir (still with lots of music). Sometimes you get endless pages about *Kraftwerk* or Keith Jarrett, and wonder if he's really just talking to his father, or maybe just using the opportunity to dissociate. This anger also manifests in a fierce defence of his working-class background. This is partly to ward off a perceived new wave of crusaders who masquerade as liberals, and who perpetuate what he describes as 'the unfair treatment of the poor'. In this light, the book is a testament to who he is, and a sort of withering rebuke against anyone (including his own readers) who might accuse him of speaking from (white male) privilege. The absolute nadir are woke (mostly middle-class) liberals who pay expensive tuition on MFA courses and write post-modern poetry – though he presumably teaches them every day and they probably also buy his books.

The best bits of the book in fact aren't about settling scores; they are the memories themselves. The most detailed episode is a schizophrenic breakdown in Paterson's late teens – an event he's speaking about for the first time in print, but whose trauma, we infer, silently informed his poetic awakening. Here all the chaotic elements in his life (drug use, emotional abuse from narcissists, debt, sexual violence) culminate in a single collapse. The perceived emptiness at his core allows for many competing voices, any of which could be the real 'him': 'at the centre of us is not a self, but a clean hole: It can be a pit, or it can be the well from which we raise the clear water of nothingness.' This feels a bit like Eliot's breakdown on Margate Sands: 'I can connect / Nothing with nothing.' But perhaps surprisingly, in sections reminiscent of *One Flew Over the Cuckoo's Nest*, Paterson's warmest descriptions are of those who are mentally ill. First there's 'Davie the Faker' who performs his own insanity to escape from his terrifying wife; then Paterson, deeply ill, gets a serene and unexpected visit from the otherwise-mute Bob on his endless corridor circuit: 'We'll see you at the other side'.

Other sections are comedy gold – something we don't often get in Paterson's oeuvre. He has a penchant for the fringe characters who make a profound and lasting impression. There's Willie at Baldragon Secondary School who is so good at drawing animals that he stuns his tormentors into 'astonished respect': 'That's... fucksakes, that's really good, Wullie'. Much later on we meet Eddie the session drummer who sets up only when the gig is about to start: 'Eddie insisted he could set up and play at the same time. Since he couldn't play at all, this seemed unlikely, but he gamely started hitting things with one hand while assembling the rest of his kit with the other.' Eddie proudly finishes setting up halfway through the gig, only to then start packing up again for another concert: 'By the end of the gig he was twatting on the cymbal, with the rest of the kit in pieces'. As ever, we wonder where these people go.

But Paterson's always been more interested in dreamy silences than in actual things. He describes a twelve-string guitar: 'two guitars emerge from the shape of one guitar. They can be slightly out of tune and even more beautiful, as the detuning causes a chorusing effect' – he could almost be talking about a lyric poem here, where the dynamics might shift, only to reveal some synaesthesic or Fibonacci principle. In the same vein, he describes his dreams: 'Again and again, laid like a weightless dimension on the heavy world, the spaces. A space will open unannounced, with a feeling of huge melancholy, passing, aftermath, intolerable beauty, yearning, an articulated mystery that speaks in late shadow and in gold light, grass and hill and sky and passing cloud.'

This sounds a bit like the film *Arrival* – with its uncanny forms and silent languages – but also echoes Paterson's comment in the preface, 'I somatise my distress and I nurture my symptoms': one wonders if his dreams have anything to do with trauma, whether the spaces are really just creases inside his body for unprocessed emotion. Perhaps they're linked to the pared-down 'nothingness' of his breakdown, or, in spiritual terms, the contemplative ambivalence we get with Antonio Machado or Rilke – bleak but affirmative at the same time.

The book twists back into nerdy analyses of jazz lineups from the 1980s, and ultimately follows its own unpredictable course, almost as though it were intended for someone else – his father, perhaps. This is on the one hand a bit frustrating: he's diving, once again, out of sight, either losing interest in his main narrative, or trying to lose our interest – we've seen too much. But this is also true to form, because, well, he warned us in the preface that this might not be his thing: 'We are not wired to identify with ourselves. I mean: it would be unbearable if all that stuff actually happened to us.' Fittingly, he said in a recent *Guardian* interview that since writing the memoir he'd 'lost interest' in it altogether. Perhaps this is true. We await the next one.

Here We Are

Lewis Warsh, *Elixir* (Ugly Duckling Presse) $20
Reviewed by Daniel Kane

Lewis Warsh (1944–2020) was inspired as much by Frank O'Hara's 'I do this, I do that' style as he was indebted to Gertrude Stein's experimental life writing. That said, from his earliest works to the posthumous collection *Elixir*, Warsh's poetry sounded like no one else's.

Take the very first poem in *Elixir*, titled 'Night Sky'. It opens with the oddly funny tercet 'Night-life in the country, / beyond the sighting / of a raccoon'. These lines are essentially a loaded and cartoonishly absurd question. What, we are asked implicitly, might constitute the essence of night-life in the country 'beyond' the mere sighting of a raccoon? The poet, these lines propose, will lead us forward by showing what is possible beyond our own limited imaginations.

Humour however is complicated by a sensuous and simultaneously melancholy emphasis on sound. For example, the repetition of the word 'night' that opens seven out of the twelve stanzas creates a practically incantatory effect. 'Night-life in the country'; 'night life in the treetops'; 'night-time in the'; 'Night-life in the Bronx'; 'Night-life on the Pacific'; 'Night-life anywhere filled'; 'Night-life in the baggage'. Stanzas six and seven revel in the sonic pleasures of place names and consonants:

North train
arrives in Wassaic, I get
off at the last stop.

Tuesday matinees
at the Triplex. The forklift
operator's wife at the end
of the bar.

Words here are as important for their percussive and

slant-rhyming effects as they are for their signifying qualities. Warsh is a poet who excels at revealing the interstices between sense and non-sense, inviting readers to delight in the pleasures of words such as 'Wassaic' and 'Triplex' while still taking care to limn the pathos of the commonplace with great tenderness. Consider the practically noirish image of 'The forklift / operator's wife at the end / of the bar'. It's a scene that is narratively separate but affectively close to both the bleak feel of the speaker getting off at the 'last stop' and the (probably sparsely attended) 'Tuesday matinées / at the Triplex'. Such lines invite comparison to characters populating Edward Hopper's 'Nighthawks' or John Cassavetes's films – people existentially alone in otherwise manifestly social situations, disconnected syntactically, prosodically, in real life.

Elixir also features poems representative of what we might call Warsh's late style – paratactic lines that critic Andy Fitch has characterized succinctly as 'deadpan juxtapositions'. Look, for instance, to the opening lines to Warsh's poem 'Last Judgement':

> You might think The Last Judgement is already at hand
> Even if you make your escape, there's no where to go
> She interrupted me as soon as I started talking
> My credit card is invalid, my arm is in a sling
> The landscape rolls by, even when you're sleeping
> I wouldn't call if it wasn't an emergency
> You can go into the corner and sulk like a baby

This assemblage-style arrangement of lines that we find here and in other poems in *Elixir* such as 'Here We Are' and 'Anything You Say' tell no story, though they do sing a seductive, intimate and simultaneously 'deadpan' song. To read *Elixir* as the book ranges across lyric, reportage, diaristic writing and dizzying parataxis is not a process of comprehending distinct poems with paraphrasable cores. Rather, it is a process of entering and revelling in an environment rich in whimsy, affection and sweet befuddlement in response to the strangeness of the everyday. *Elixir* is a wonderful introduction to Warsh's work as it is a sustaining treat for his long-time fans.

First as Tragedy, Then as Farce

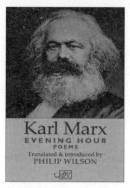

Karl Marx, *Evening Hour,* translated and introduced by Philip Wilson (Arc Publications) £8
Amanda Dalton, *Notes on Water* (Smith Doorstop) £6.50
Martin Stannard, *Postcards to Ma* (Leafe Press) £6
Reviewed by Rory Waterman

Readers won't be surprised that Karl Marx was an appalling poet, though they might be surprised by the kind of appalling poet he was. As Philip Wilson tells us in the helpful introduction to this dual-language selection of eleven poems from an extant haul of 120, 'The young Marx dreamed of a career as a man of letters. He wrote poetry prolifically for two years', also found time to pen a novel and a verse tragedy, and eventually came to the judicious conclusion that he 'lacked the talent'. Most of the poems in *Evening Hour* are tightly formal, wholly conventional, and inherently boring. Wilson is generous in his faint praise: 'The verse comes across as very competent pastiche: the ballads and the love lyrics ventriloquise Friedrich von Schiller and Heinrich Heine'. The following will serve as an example, and I have not cherry-picked an especially naff passage:

> Do you know the magic fulness,
> When souls flow out to meet each other,
> And pour themselves in exhalation,
> In melody and friendliness?

Souls pop up like molehills all over the neat little lawns of Marx's poems, which is perhaps surprising when one considers his maxim – more memorable than any lines of his verse – that religion is *das Opium des Volkes*. Indeed, there are few indications in this work of Marx as we know him. The closest he gets, at least in this selection, is a satirical epigram, which begins: 'In his armchair, cosy and stupid, / Sits silently our German public'. The poem never homes in as one might expect, though, but instead sails loftily, from where it can hit no marks. A short pamphlet of his poetry will be enough to sate anyone's curiosity – but isn't it intriguing to know Marx wrote like this, once? His poetry really did make nothing happen, and had he stuck to his initial ambitions, the past century of world history might have been rather different.

In (at least) one of Richmal Crompton's later William stories, written while bastardisations of Marx's non-poetic ideas were controlling the lives of half of the world's population, the dishevelled eleven-year-old hero sits scowling at his school desk while holding a book upside down in front of him, and receives the telling off he no doubt deserves. He should've picked up Amanda Dalton's *Notes on Water*, both covers of which are front covers, and which contains two long poems bearing that title; after reading one, you turn the pamphlet upside down and start at the beginning again on the other.

One poem begins in dream or fever-dream, we don't initially know which (though that soon becomes apparent):

> I'm swimming in an artificial pool
> inside a broken building.
> the water is deep and brown
> and full of wreckage.

The poem's tight sections, separated by asterisks, then move between multivalently watery scenarios: the 'smiling boy in the car park, / little Noah, pouring rivers from a watering can', the flood 'that made the whole town one big filthy river; floating cars on Albert Street, St George's Square an artificial lake'. 'Next day the fucking sightseers block the streets. // Next day the water sings.' Stitched throughout the poem is the speaker's sister, 'kneeling in the rubble', and 'the man who will leave in winter'. The poem coheres, and is moving and evocative, but I don't want to ruin it for you. In its counterpart, a horrible, wonderful poem of memory, loss, love, pain, 'a woman waits through a long night' while a man upstairs 'lies soaked in pain / but still the doctor doesn't come'. It is all original in the telling if not in the tale, and the formatting is no gimmick: the two poems meet, joltingly, in the middle. *This* is poetry.

But then poetry is many things. Sumer is ycumen in, and Martin Stannard's *Postcards to Ma*, one twelve-page stanza, is the beach read you didn't know you need. Not really – but also, why not? The poem's comically tortured, self-absorbed, Beckettian hero is on a solitary holiday (the bed is 'pleasingly firm Back / can't stand nights on anything too squishy One reason / I left wife') somewhere sun-soaked and sea-splashed, from where he sends daily postcards to Ma. The poem doesn't comprise these postcards, but is instead a frenetic, surreal, virtually unpunctuated fourteen-days-in-the-life. On day three, having arrived in 'Horse-hauled taxi cart', checked in, 'Slept like a library book nobody wants to read', sent the obligatory postcard to Ma, photographed everything and everyone in sight ('Especially receptionist in crisp / white blouse and cosmetics'), walked around town, again slept ('like a folded sheep') and 'Frolicked on sand' (another daily dalliance), he turns his attention to the local hospital and to curing 'loads of patients' of 'lupus shingles psoriasis schizophrenia (had to cure that / one twice) herpes scabies' etc, before sleeping 'like a patient etherised in a 4-star stable'.

You get the idea, but it seems apposite to go on anyway. A few days later, after an afternoon spent reading philosophers, from Socrates to Hobbes (of course) to Kierkegaard (also of course) to Superman (once more: of course – and yes, Nietzsche directly beforehand), he sleeps 'like a monk in a convent'. As the fortnight draws to a close, he finds time to acquire a BA and an MA, to learn a plethora of instruments ('piano violin cello guitar ukulele flute / piccolo trumpet bassoon oboe recorder harmonica ket-

tle / drum triangle'), and to write a symphony, two sonatas, three violin concertos, 'some songs', two novels and a 'slim volume of award-winning poetry / *The Zenith of Our Feelings* When a man is happy / he writes damn good poetry'. He hasn't seemed especially happy most of the time; but if your brain blinks while you're reading this poem, you might miss many of its barbed little jokes. 'Could be making all this up', he later confesses. Perhaps the only thing that could make this rollicking poem any more enjoyable would be a facsimile of a postcard at the end: 'Dear Ma, Having a lovely relaxing time. Lots of love…'.

Write dirty words

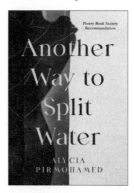

Alycia Pirmohamed, *Another Way to Split Water* (Polygon) £10; Jenni Fagan, *The Bone Library* £10 (Polygon)
Reviewed by Aoife Lyall

Another Way to Split Water is filled with the shapeshifting bodies of land, water and woman: bodies of blood and myth, bequest and second sight. While Pirmohamed interrogates the place of woman as migrant, daughter and lover, the caveats of 'another', 'after', and 'elsewhere' fill the collection, denying the singular, linear narratives that have defined these identities, and our relationship to them, for so long.

Part I speaks both to a pervasive sense of want, 'lately, I read about storms all night / because there is no lightning here' ('Meditation While Plaiting My Hair') and, significantly, the uncertainty that follows the fulfilment of want, through the 'stammer of lightning' in 'Nights / Flatline'. The poems trace a speaker desperate to understand her individual self 'I titled another page with my body / and sundered every bending, splitting line of myself / to the making' ('Hinge') before the revelation that hers are inherent, and inherited, divisions:

> but one day I'll split into myth
>
> and pass through the mouths of a hundred generations.
> I am woman after woman after spooling
>
> woman […]
> ('The Fish that Halved Water')

In poems such as 'After the House of Wisdom', the speaker pulls these external, fractured states inwards, becoming their source rather than their outcome:

Perhaps it is the other way around, small
rivers uncoiling into ink on this version
of my eyes. So, I rinse in a bath of citations,
[...]
unfolding my spine in one long extended verse.

This new perspective brings forth the declaration 'This is me, driving straight / into my own life,' in 'Self-addressed' and the revelation in 'Midnight Vessel Across the Great Sea', that 'inheritance is a form / of second sight... My second sight is an heirloom'.

Pirmohamed's Part II opens with 'Welcome', its first line an undercurrent that undermines the sure footedness of the previous poems: 'You know better than to feel welcome at anything resembling a border'. And so here, as in 'Elsewhere', and 'Persephone's Crossings' we are presented with opened wounds, jagged edges, the darkness and fragments of change and displacement:

Even as a young girl, you found fragments
of the broken mirror that same country handed you

in which you saw not your own reflection
but something jagged, something too dark, too dark,
too dark.

The land is not an objective, external factor, but intrinsically bound to the body that inhabits it 'In the blood of every migrant / there is a map pointing home' ('My Body is a Forest'), a sentiment which can both support and subvert the migrant's delicate balance of belonging: 'I envy birds / that pump blood according to instinct, / never concerning themselves with the bloodline threading through.' ('Avian Circulatory System').

It is in water, full of its others and anothers, that the speaker finds respite, hope, and restitution. It is in rivers, not roots, movement not stillness, that a sense of self begins to form 'where her body is shaped like the river / and the river // is shaped like belonging'. ('Elsewhere') Reminiscent of Natalie Diaz, Rachael Allen, Eiléan Ni Chuilleanáin, and Nidhi Zak,

Pirmohamed is a writer of multitudes and *Another Way to Split Water* is a collection that surges with tumultuous power and purpose.

*

The Bone Library echoes with vibrant poems of love and life, art and death. It refuses to bow to solemnity and gravitas, instead espousing anger, kindness, and vivacity in generous measures.

Fagan gives voice to the bewildered and enraged masses through frequent colloquialisms and obscenities, '... this world / held hostage by fucking mentalists / sorting

out this shit'. ('The Nineteen Thirties House'). Knowing the traditional expectation of libraries and governments alike- for members to be quiet, biddable, and subservient- Fagan takes great joy in rattling the old bones, 'Write dirty words / big! Coarse as possible, // and always – underline them'. ('Your Sexts are Shit'), using art to amplify rather than subjugate the unrefined fury felt with each new debasement of human dignity, each new insult to those already struggling to cope under current economic and political regimes. 'I know who I am – / and who I am / is not beholden to wankers' ('I Know Who I am').

Fagan knows how to set a scene, dress a set, and tell a story, and her poems fill the inanimate space of the library with dramatic, theatrical flourishes:

I sleep on the sofa
for months (in that dress)
with a baseball bat

beside me,
cos junkies flame-balled
my window

trying to create
a crack den with a view,
till I took over,
('It was an Ex-Council House on the Sea Wall,
Graffiti All Over It)

These poems refuse to be catalogued, jumping from wolves to urinals, decomposing sheep heads to Catherine Wheels, with imagery as animated as it is distinct: 'She wasn't a starfish exactly, there were bits of me she wanted' ('I told her'), and 'instead of flowers / you sent flying moths // to eat my visions'. ('Penrose Stairs'); with an energy that fully endorses her belief that 'the best art / restarts the atriums' ('The Good Stuff').

On the subject of art, Fagan takes the reader right to the beautiful, tortured heart of it when she writes:

it's hard

to make art
out of darkness

and bind it,
with your own soul's light.
('Summerhall Almanac')

The Bone Library is a curio in itself. Bringing Fagan's experience as a novelist and playwright to the fore, it gives the reader a diverse and captivating collection to experience and envisage.

Some Contributors

Bedilu Wakjira is Assistant Professor of Linguistics at Addis Ababa University in Ethiopia. He has published short stories, essays and five collections of poetry in Amharic.

Chris Beckett's latest publications are *Tenderfoot* (Carcanet, 2020) and as editor/translator, *Songs We Learn from Trees* (Carcanet, 2020) which was a finalist in the Glenna Luschei Prize for African Poetry, 2021.

Peter Robinson is a professor of literature at the University of Reading, and poetry editor for *The Fortnightly Review*. His most recent collection is *Retrieved Attachments* (Two Rivers Press, 2023).

Jenny King was born in London in 1940 and lives in Sheffield, where The Poetry Business published her pamphlets *Tenants* and *Midsummer*. Her collection *Moving Day* was published by Carcanet in 2021.

Grevel Lindop has published six collections of poems with Carcanet, most recently *Luna Park* (2017), as well as biographies of De Quincey and Charles Williams. His website is at www.grevel.co.uk

Silis MacLeod was born on the Isle of Harris to a crofting family. She worked as a municipal librarian for most of her life. She is retired and lives in her grandfather's house.

Christian Wiman's new book, *Zero at the Bone: Fifty Entries Against Despair*, will be published in December by Farrar, Straus and Giroux.

Richard Price's next Carcanet collection *Late Gifts* will be published in October. Its theme is the demanding and joyful relationship between a middle-aged father and his new son – and the urgent environmental issues of their present and future.

Anthony (Vahni) Capildeo is a Trinidadian Scottish writer of poetry and non-fiction. Their work includes *Like a Tree, Walking* (Carcanet, 2021). They are Writer in Residence at the University of York.

Declan Ryan's first book, *Crisis Actor*, is published by Faber & Faber in July.

Paul Franz's poems appear in *Berfrois*, *Prelude* and the *New York Review of Books*.

Daniel Kane is professor of American literature at Uppsala University. His publications include *Do You Have a Band? Poetry and Punk Rock in New York City* (2017), *We Saw the Light: Conversations Between the New American Cinema and Poetry* (2009) and *All Poets Welcome: The Lower East Side Poetry Scene in the 1960s* (2003).

Christian Wethered is a poet and songwriter based in Dublin. His work has featured in *Poetry Ireland Review*, *Poetry Wales*, *The Belfield Literary Review* and *The Moth*.

Caroline Sylge's poetry is published in *New Poetries*, *PN Review*, *Stand*, *Ambit*, *The Independent* and *Ink, Sweat and Tears*. She is a writer and the founder of The Global Retreat Company.

Christina Buckton was an educationist and therapist before focusing seriously on poetry in her eighties, publishing her collection *Holding it Together* in 2022. She died, aged eighty-six, in January 2023.

Editors
Michael Schmidt
John McAuliffe

Editorial Manager
Andrew Latimer

Contributing Editors
Vahni Capildeo
Sasha Dugdale
Will Harris

Copyeditor
Maren Meinhardt

Designer
Andrew Latimer

Editorial address
The Editors at the address on the right. Manuscripts cannot be returned unless accompanied by a stamped addressed envelope or international reply coupon.

Trade distributors
NBN International

Represented by
Compass IPS Ltd

Copyright
© 2023 Poetry Nation Review
All rights reserved
ISBN 978-1-80017-370-5
ISBN 0144-7076

Subscriptions—6 issues
INDIVIDUAL–print and digital:
£45; abroad £65
INSTITUTIONS–print only:
£76; abroad £90
INSTITUTIONS–digital only:
from Exact Editions (https://shop.exacteditions.com/gb/pn-review)
to: PN Review, Alliance House,
30 Cross Street, Manchester,
M2 7AQ, UK.

Supported by

Supported using public funding by
ARTS COUNCIL ENGLAND